A Future and a Hope

Sermons of Comfort
in
Seasons of Confusion

A Future and a Hope
Jon Courson
Applegate Christian Fellowship
Jacksonville, Oregon

All Scripture taken from the King James Version

We are

TROUBLED ON EVERY SIDE, YET NOT DISTRESSED . . .

PERPLEXED, BUT NOT IN DESPAIR . . .

PERSECUTED, BUT NOT FORSAKEN . . .

CAST DOWN, BUT NOT DESTROYED . . .

ALWAYS BEARING ABOUT IN THE BODY THE DYING OF THE LORD JESUS, THAT THE LIFE ALSO OF JESUS MIGHT BE MADE MANIFEST IN OUR BODY.

II CORINTHIANS 4:8-10

IT HAS rightly been said that 'a sermon born in the head reaches the head; but a sermon born in the heart reaches the heart.' That is why our Lord allows His children to go through heartaches and heartbreaks from time to time. You see, He comes to us during such seasons in a most wonderful way, and then He flows through us, enabling us to help others in their trials and tragedies with the insights and understandings we've been given.

This is precisely what the Apostle Paul proclaimed when he said, 'Blessed be God, even the Father of our Lord Jesus Christ, the Father of mercies, and the God of all comfort; who comforteth us in all our tribulation, that we may be able to comfort them which are in any trouble, by the comfort wherewith we ourselves are comforted of God' (II Corinthians 1:3-4).

He comforts us that we might comfort others. And such is the purpose of this book — that people like you who are going through, or who will go through, trials and tragedies, might discover what I've discovered in my own situation: Our Father is absolutely faithful; the Savior is so very real; and the Spirit is so incredibly comforting in times of trials.

The following studies span a period of 15 years. Some of the insights were immediate at the time of the trials. Others evolved over a few years — similar to the way a photograph becomes slowly clearer in the process of development. All were originally shared with the prayer that these studies would be more than theoretical or theological. My hope was that they would be incarnational in order that the family at Applegate would see the Word become flesh as they experienced the undeniable Presence of Jesus in our midst.

And such is my prayer for you — that in whatever trial you may be personally, you might come to see Jesus ever more clearly.

When Bad Things Happen to Good People

Therefore whosoever heareth these sayings of mine, and doeth them, I will liken him unto a wise man, which built his house upon a rock: And the rain descended, and the floods came, and the winds blew, and beat upon that house; and it fell not: for it was founded upon a rock. And every one that heareth these sayings of mine, and doeth them not, shall be likened unto a foolish man, which built his house upon the sand: And the rain descended, and the floods came, and the winds blew, and beat upon that house; and it fell: and great was the fall of it.

Matthew 7:24-27

SEVERAL EVENINGS this week, NBC Nightly News reported the Mickey Leland story — the account of the Congressman who flew to Ethiopia to research United States assistance in the Ethiopian famine. If you have been following the story, you know that the airplane crashed and Mickey Leland, along with several others, was killed. NBC aired a brief segment of his memorial service, and the words of the minister who conducted the service really caught my attention. He said, 'Why good people experience tragedy, I can't say. Why bad things happen to good people, I don't know.'

This statement has been stirring in my mind for some time now. Why do bad things happen to good people? Are there no answers? Whether it's concerning Mickey Leland in Ethiopia, or your own situation of the past week or two, people always ask the question: Why do bad things happen to good people?

Two years ago, a best-selling book was entitled just that: Why Bad Things Happen To Good People. The author concluded there are no real answers; even as there are no easy answers. I suggest to you, however, that there is a profoundly simple answer to this question: There are no good people.

> *There is none righteous, no, not one. There is*
> *none that understandeth, there is none that*

seeketh after God. They are all gone out of the
way, they are together become unprofitable.
There is none that doeth good, no, not one.

Romans 3:10-12

You see, the world thinks, 'I'm OK, you're OK.' But regardless of what psychologists tell us, this just isn't so. For those who look to worldly understandings and explanations miss the central truth: There are no good people. So the real question is not 'Why do bad things happen to good people?' but 'Why do good things happen to bad people?' You might have had a bad day or a terrible time this last month or two, but what we deserve is to live in terror, in tragedy, in difficulty every day of our lives because there is none that is good, not one.

'Why, then,' we sometimes wonder, 'are good things happening to those people who live next to me? They're not in church today — they're out on the lake water skiing. Yet they get the raises and promotions. Why do good things happen to them?' Because, God is good.

The first verse my kids learn is Psalm 73:1: 'God is good,' followed by 1 John 4:16: 'God is love' because I'm convinced that the fundamental, foundational concepts we need to embrace ourselves and pass on to others concern the goodness and the love of God. He is a loving Father who causes His sun to rise on the evil and on the good, sending rain upon the crops of the just and the unjust (Matthew 5:45). God loves to bless people because He is good.

John Claypool was right when he said, 'God is the victim of bad PR, usually propagated by those who know Him.' Too often, believers and unbelievers alike generate the false idea that, although God occasionally does a good thing, basically He's mean. We hear sermons and testimonies to that effect, saying, 'God got hold of me when He broke my legs and took away my house and caused me to go bankrupt.' That's not Father God — that's the Godfather!

Listen carefully, gang. One of the great frustrations I have in talking with unbelievers is their impression that they have to wait until their marriage is on the rocks, until their finances are crumbling, or until cancer is eating them up before they will consider Christ. They think their lives have to fall apart before they turn to Jesus. So, to the person who's skiing on the lake today behind his power boat, outside his 2,000-square-foot cabin we shouldn't say, 'God's going to get you' — but 'Hasn't God been *good* to you?'

The Bible says God demonstrated His love for us all in that while we were yet sinners, Christ died for us (Romans 5:8); but people in the world today have lost this understanding. In my hometown of San Jose, one of my friends went into a jewelry store to buy a necklace for his wife. 'You want a cross?' asked the clerk. 'Yes,' my friend answered. And the clerk said, 'Do you want a plain cross, or the one with the little man on it?' People don't understand that Jesus' death was a demonstration of God's love for all people — that God desired to bless us even while we were still sinners. God looked at J. Paul Getty, the oil billionaire, and said, 'I'm going to bless you, Mr. Getty.' When Getty was asked about the key to his success, he said, 'Rise up early. Work hard. Strike oil.' Getty attributed none of his success to God, but God blessed him anyway. God blessed J.D. Rockefeller, who, while reading the book of Genesis, came across the story of Noah using pitch to seal the ark. Rockefeller said, 'Pitch? Hmm. That means petroleum.' He sent a team to the Middle East, became a multi-billionaire, and founded the largest oil company in world history. God blessed him in spite of the fact that there is no indication Rockefeller acted on any other portion of Scripture, save the story of Noah and the ark.

It rains on the just and the unjust. The sun shines on the believer and the unbeliever because God is good. Everything He gives us is because of grace — unmerited, undeserved, unearned favor. But if we don't recognize this, if we misinterpret the source of our blessings, we become narrow and bitter and full of sorrow. Failing to acknowledge the goodness of God in blessing him with his millions, J. Paul Getty in his later years became so tight and stingy he wouldn't ever buy a meal. He took a sack lunch to work and wouldn't even plop down a buck for a burger. 'Too expensive,' he said as he died in isolation and misery. J.D. Rockefeller, when asked at the end of his life how much money it takes to satisfy a man, answered, 'Just a little more.'

In our text, Jesus says a day is coming when the rains will fall and the winds shall beat on the house of every man. Of what storm is He speaking? Death. The statistics are conclusive: ten out of ten people die. Every person who has ever lived since Jesus spoke these words has built his house and done his thing until the storm came — at which point it was determined whether he had built upon the rock or upon the sand. Jesus ended His Sermon on the Mount speaking of two roads: one unto life, one unto destruction; two trees: one of fruitfulness, one of failure; two foundations: one to stand, one to collapse. The choice is yours. Upon which foundation will you build?

'Wait,' you say. 'I have one more question. If God is our good Father, why does He allow the devil to inflict pain and disease, destruction and death, discouragement and difficulties? Can't God stop the devil and put an end to our misery?' Yes, He can. And yes, He will. But presently, God allows storms to arise, which will test our foundation, in order that we might see where we stand eternally.

In response to a growing demand for their product, East Coast cod fishermen began to ship frozen cod all over the country. They discovered one drawback, however. In the freezing process, the cod lost its flavor. To remedy this, the fishermen shipped their cod live in salt-water tanks to be processed once they reached their destination. The fish arrived OK, but because they were sitting in these tanks, they became spongy and soft. For several years, the fishermen didn't know what to do. Then someone had a brilliant idea: Ship the fish in salt-water tanks, but throw in some catfish — the natural enemy of the codfish. They tried it. The catfish chased the codfish all around the tank as they traveled cross-country, and when the codfish arrived, those that made it alive were flavorful and were sold at premium prices. The catfish were necessary to keep the codfish moving, thereby enhancing their texture and flavor. So, too, God says to us, 'Because I want the best for you both now and in eternity, I will allow an occasional catfish to come into your tank and chase you around for a little while. Otherwise, you'll just sit around and get soft. But I will not test you above that which you are able (1 Corinthians 10:13). And I will always be with you (Matthew 28:20). Call upon Me in the day of trouble

(Psalm 50:15). And cast your care upon Me (1 Peter 5:7). All things are working together for good (Romans 8:28). Trust Me' (Psalm 37:3).

Build your life on the Rock, gang. Jesus is a sure Foundation and He won't let you down.

Only a Test

And it came to pass after these things, that God did tempt Abraham, and said unto him, Abraham: and he said, Behold, here I am. And he said, Take now thy son, thine only son Isaac, whom thou lovest, and get thee into the land of Moriah; and offer him there for a burnt offering upon one of the mountains which I will tell thee of.

Genesis 22:1-2

WHAT IS God doing with you, anyway?' ' Ed asked me after hearing about the condition of my 21-year-old son, Peter John. While directing our mission school on the South Pacific Island of Vanuatu, Peter contracted malaria. A recurring 105-degree temperature brought him home for treatment. But he continued to lose weight at a radical rate — from 172 lbs. when he left for Vanuatu, to his present weight of 136. On Thursday, doctors concluded that, along with malaria, Peter had a severe case of Crohn's Disease — a disease of the intestines. According to the doctors treating him, unless the Lord intervenes, Peter will require medication for the rest of his life. He will also undergo a series of surgeries, which will more than likely result in a colostomy. So it was after hearing this news from his wife, who is a nurse at the hospital where Peter John is being treated, that Ed — a new believer — asked his pointed question: 'What is God doing with you, anyway?'

And I found myself saying something which I knew to be, oh, so true as I answered, 'Listen to me very carefully, Ed. This is a test. It's only a test.' If you're old enough, like me, you can remember the high-pitched tone that would occasionally appear on the TV screen, along with a voice saying, 'This is a test. This is only a test. If this were an actual emergency, you would be instructed to. . .'

So, too, according to our text, God tested Abraham. 'But my Bible reads, God *tempted* Abraham,' you might say. Keep in mind that the word 'test' and 'tempt' are used interchangeably in the Bible because, linguistically, they're the same word. Therefore, what God means for a test, Satan seeks to use as a temptation to bring us into despair, discouragement, defeat or depression. Conversely, what Satan means as a temptation, God uses as a test to show us how He'll come through.

When did God test Abraham? After *these* things (Genesis 22:1). After what things? After 60 years of preparation. Our wonderful Father, our Master Mentor, painstakingly prepared Abraham for the time when He would ask Abraham to sacrifice his son on Mt. Moriah. Sixty years previously, God had called Abraham to leave his comfortable life in Ur. On his way to the land God would show him, Abraham buried his father and almost lost his wife on two occasions due to his unbelief (Genesis 12, 20). He lost his nephew when Lot moved to Sodom, and lost his son when he sent Ishmael away (Genesis 21).

All of these events were part of the Father's curriculum to prepare Abraham for the Moriah moment — just as He prepares us for every test we ever face . . .

An Open-Book Test

I can still feel the sweat on my brow and the knot in my stomach whenever Dr. Flanner, my physics teacher, said, 'Put your name on top of your paper. This is a test.' But I always breathed a sigh of relief whenever he said, 'This is an open-book test.' You see, if you've been in school awhile, you know a secret about textbooks which is also true of the Bible: the answers are all in the back of the Book. Therefore, as I turn to the back of the Bible — to the Book of Revelation — I find the ultimate answer for every test I will ever face: heaven. In heaven, there will be no more tears, no more trials, no more tests. And, Christian, that's where we're all headed.

Not only is the ultimate answer at the back of the Book, but hints of the answer are scattered throughout, including, 'All things work together for good to those that love God' (Romans 8:28). The word 'all' in Greek is an interesting one. It doesn't mean a few, or some, or most. It means *all*. Therefore, the answer to any test we face lies in the fact that *everything* works together for good to any who love God and are called by Him.

A Group-Discussion Test

Happy the day when Dr. Flanner would say, 'Get in groups of four for an open-book, group-discussion test.' That's the kind of test the Father gives us. You see, God doesn't say, 'Here's a test, Jon. Face this trial, this temptation, this problem — and I'll be back in an hour to grade you. Good luck.' No! There's a whole 'Group' taking the test with me . . .

The Holy Spirit is within me;

the Son is right beside me;

the Father gives the answers to me.

As the Assyrians threatened them, the people of Judah said, 'We know the answer: We'll get the Egyptians to help us.' 'Woe be to you, rebellious children,' God said in response. 'You take counsel, but not of Me.' Then God went on to say, 'If you turn to Me, you will hear a voice in your ear saying, This is the way, walk ye in it, when ye turn to the right, and when ye turn to the left' (Isaiah 30).

So, too, in the trial I go through, in the test you may be in, if we face it alone, we'll fall. But if we take the test in the midst of our 'Group' — the Trinity — there's absolutely no way we'll fail.

Pass/Pass

Not only does the Father painstakingly prepare us for the tests we face; provide the answers in His Word; position us in a group with the Trinity — but He promises we'll pass. Dear saint, the test before you is not pass/fail. It's pass/pass. How do I know? Look at our text. It says, 'After these things came to *pass* . . .' (Genesis 22:1).

'Being confident of this very thing,' Paul would later write, 'that He who began a good work in you *will* perform it until the day of Jesus Christ' (Philippians 1:6). In other words, God is saying, 'The blood of My Son was shed for you that you might be part of My family. I've made a huge investment to see you make it through. Therefore, I *know* you'll pass this test.'

A Test-imony

'I'm tired of this test,' you might be saying. There's only one way to end it: be like Abraham. Pass it! Then, like Abraham, you will not only pass your test, but you will emerge with a test-imony. You see, directly following his Moriah moment, Abraham received fresh revelation of God as evidenced by the new name by which he referred to God: Jehovah-Jireh, the God Who Provides (Genesis

22:14). Abraham came to know God in a way he hadn't known Him before as a result of the test he underwent.

Why is it that some Bible teaching is powerful and impacting, while the same exact message, given by someone else, is devoid of power and anointing? It's because sermons, which are born in the head, only reach other heads. It takes a sermon born in one's heart and borne out through one's life to touch other hearts and lives. In any particular message, you may not 'give your testimony'; but if you've lived through the passage, if you've experienced it in some way, there will be an incarnational nature to it — human flesh embodying God's Spirit — which will impact hearts and touch lives. The power lies in allowing the message to become incarnational, the doctrine to become reality, the Word to become flesh.

To Thomas, who at last joined the other disciples in the Upper Room, Jesus didn't say, 'Let Me explain to you the seven points of Resurrection Reality, alliterated and outlined.' He said, 'Touch My wounds' (John 20:27). Likewise, whenever we allow people to see our hurts and failings, the skeptics in our midst change their minds. 'Your God must truly be God,' they say. 'You were wounded deeply, but you're still standing. You were hit by tragedy, but you're going on. You were wiped out physically, but your countenance shines brightly.'

And so it was that I could say, 'Ed, I gotta tell you — it's only a test. The Lord has faithfully prepared me, and He'll do the same for you. He's given us the Answer Book, the Ultimate Discussion Group, and a guarantee that we'll pass.'

A Future and a Hope

Our God is so good, gang. I promise you, whatever test comes your way, He has already prepared you and will continue to see you through in order that you may emerge with a testimony which will impact many.

Glorying in Tribulation

And not only so, but we glory in tribulations also...

Romans 5:3

THE APOSTLE Paul's middle name could well have been 'Trouble.' Wherever he went, whatever he said caused difficulty and controversy. Think you had a tough time this week? Think about Paul. From the time he became a minister of the Gospel he was: put to hard labor, beaten, imprisoned, given 39 lashes five times, stoned, shipwrecked three times, stranded a day and a night in the open ocean, and left for dead. When Paul talked about difficulties, he knew from whence he spoke. Yet he said we not only rejoice in coming glory, but in present tribulations. Why? Because tribulation is the catalyst God uses to bring about patience, experience, and hope. We see this principle in nature . . .

The Seventeen-Mile Drive on the Monterey Peninsula is world-famous for, among other things, the beautiful cypress trees that abound in that region. Because of their beauty, these cypress trees are photographed, painted, and sculpted by artists from all over the world. I find it fascinating that the reason they're so beautiful is due to the wind that blows them constantly. I am intrigued by the fact that the wind produces outward beauty, but also develops inward strength. You see, the root system of the cypress trees sinks proportionately deeper than that of any other tree in the state, which is especially interesting considering the mighty redwood also makes California its home.

'Lord, I want to be an object of beauty,' we say. 'Alright,' He says, and proceeds to send winds of adversity, not to blow us out, but to make us beautiful. The cold winds of adversity, the hot winds of tribulation, cause us to sink our root systems deeper in the soil of Scripture, to ground and root us in faith. That's why Paul says we are to rejoice in tribulations. Truly, they make us not only more beautiful, but they make us strong.

Tribulations and testing are what God uses to take the dings and dents out of our body — both corporately and individually. God takes us into His body shop. He starts pounding away, pulling out dents, and doing some grinding. Gang, it's not during the party times when strength is developed, when beauty is born. It's when the wind is howling and the sander humming that God is doing His finishing work. Ask Johann Sebastian Bach . . .

This man, who was one of the most prolific composers of history, locked himself in a room, day after day, where he put pen to paper and scored the glorious compositions he heard in his mind. Why did he lock himself in the confines of a single room? He had twenty kids. You would lock yourself in a room too if twenty kids were running around your house! Yet from his times of testing, tribulation, and challenge came beautiful music.

Paul makes the same point, saying, 'Don't only rejoice in your peace with God, your access to God, or your hope in God, but rejoice also in your present difficulty because it's working in you something of beauty.

'I know that,' you say. 'Everyone knows we're to count it all joy when we fall into various trials. I already understand that concept.' Do you? The prophet Jeremiah was a man who knew the Lord, but he struggled with something the Lord had told him prophetically and which he observed personally. That is, the Babylonians — equivalent to the Iraqis today — would soon march on Jerusalem. When Jeremiah asked 'why,' God told him to do something very interesting. 'Arise,' He said. 'Go down to the potter's house and I will cause you to hear My words' (Jeremiah 18:2). So, Jeremiah went to the potter's house, wherein he observed clay on a potter's wheel. The most common of all substances, clay typifies you and me. Psalm 103 declares that as a father has compassion on his children, so the Lord has compassion on us, remembering our frames and knowing that we are but dust, earth, clay. God is not mad *at* us, disappointed *in* us, or tired *of* us. Knowing we're nothing more than lumps of clay, He has chosen to work *on* us.

That is why Jeremiah saw not only the clay, he saw the Master Potter as well — pumping the pedal which caused the wheel to turn. 'The problem with life,' said one philosopher, 'is that it's so daily.' Maybe you can relate to that. If you're in school it's: Geometry, History, English, and lunch. You go home, have a Twinkie, watch TV, do homework, go to bed — and get up the next morning for Geometry. If you work, it's the same old people, same old problems, and same old struggles every morning. Round and round you go, day after day. That's how the clay felt. And sometimes we become so tired of the routine of our lives that we say, 'I'm getting off this wheel.' What, then, does the Master Potter do? Even as Jeremiah observed, He picks us up — lumps of clay that we are — kneads us a bit, and puts us right back on the wheel. Listen, gang, here's the fact: All of us are aware of the 'circularness,' the sameness of every day life. But it's all part of the plan of the Potter. And, if I try and escape, I will only be crushed in the process before I end up right back where I started.

The storm raged. The disciples rowed and complained. Then they saw Jesus walking on the water. 'Lord! If that's You, bid me to come,' Peter said — perhaps not so much as an act of faith as a plea to get away from the disciples. 'Okay. Come on, Peter,' Jesus said (Matthew 14:29). And Peter got out and started walking to Jesus. But he took his eyes off the Lord, focused on the storm, and what happened to him is the same thing that happens to us: he began to sink. 'Save me Lord!' he cried. So Jesus lifted Peter, the giant fisherman, out of the water with a one-armed curl and put him where? Right back in the boat.

God puts us in fixes to fix us. If I try and fix the fix God put me in, He's got to put me in another fix to fix the fix He wanted to fix in the first place. So, slowly but surely, I'm learning to be content in the boat — to remain on the wheel. Yet, no sooner do I accept the confines and routine of my situation, than I feel the hand of the Master Potter suddenly and unexpectedly poking me, pinching me, shaping me. And if I'm not, oh, so careful, I will jump off the wheel once more — this time not because of predictability, but because of pressure. If I do, I'll find myself face-down on the floor before I feel the hand of my Master Potter picking me up, and plopping me on the wheel once again. This process may go on, over and over again, until I finally give up and lay still on the wheel. But, when I do, if I catch my reflection in the window, I'll see myself taking shape as the Potter forms me into something useful. 'Far out!' I think as the wheel comes to a stop. Then I feel the hands of the Potter under me and I think, 'This is great! Now He's going to put me on the top shelf, in a place where everyone can see me.'

But instead, He walks right by the top shelf and keeps going until I hear the sound of a door opening. It's the kiln. In I go, the door closes behind me, the temperature goes up, and I start sweating. 'What now, Lord?' I cry. 'Why am I in this place? What in the world is going on?' And He answers, 'It takes not only pressure points, but fiery trials to produce in you, Jon, a hardness so you won't crack up or flake out.' This process continues until the Potter takes me out and carries me to His shop.

Now, according to Romans 9:21, the Lord makes some vessels to honor, some to dishonor. That means He makes some people beautiful vases to hold flowers, but others He makes spittoons or toilet bowls. 'Wait a minute!' I protest. 'Let me get this straight. I should rejoice in tribulations because tribulation works patience, which produces experience, which produces hope, which makes me unashamed. But what if He is making me a spittoon? The dailiness of my job, the boringness of my career, the sameness of my school, the pressure financially, maritally, emotionally — when all is said and done, am I going to end up a toilet bowl? Is that what this is all about, Lord?

But wait. Look again at the Master Potter. In the feet pumping the pedal, which causes the wheel to turn so routinely, you will see holes where a nail pierced them for the sake of the clay. Look at the hands putting pressure on the clay. See the holes in each palm, and realize the Master Potter is the Wonderful Counselor, the Everlasting

Father, the Prince of Peace, your Savior, Jesus Christ. If He loves you so much He was willing to be pinned to the Cross, you can trust that the sameness of your schedule, and the pressure in your life is meant to make you into something wonderful.

And not only does He love you that much now, but when you were a sinner — when you were ungodly, when you were an enemy — He was in love with you (Romans 5:8). Suppose my wife, Tammy, and I go house shopping and find one for $5,000. The roof is caving in. The wires are hanging out. The floors are sagging. The foundation is gone. But Tammy loves it anyway, so I buy it. Then, unbeknownst to her, I call fifteen master carpenters and craftsmen and pay them $500,000 to replace the roof, rewire, and rework the entire house from top to bottom. Then I take Tammy back to the house, and she looks around and says, 'This is fabulous. I loved it when it was a shack, but now look at it!'

God loved you when you were a shack. He said, 'I see there's no foundation under your life, no covering over your life, no wiring in your life, but I love you just the way you are.' And because He was in love with you at your worst, you can be assured that for the rest of your life — now that you're beginning to be reworked, rewired, and rebuilt — you'll never have to doubt His love, not even for a moment.

Why am I sharing this? Because I know bunches of us understand with our minds the value of tribulation and trials. But even though we embrace the understanding theologically, we struggle with it internally and we start sniveling. 'If He loves me,' we murmur, 'why isn't He doing this thing or answering that prayer?'

Something big was about to happen. The mother of James and John could sense the excitement in the air. Indeed, in a few hours, the city would be crying, 'Hosanna! Hosanna! Blessed is the King of Israel, that cometh in the name of the Lord!' So it was that Salome came to Jesus and worshipped Him right before His triumphal entry (Matthew 20). Fully aware she was worshipping Him not out of love, but in order to manipulate Him and get what she wanted, Jesus lovingly looked at her and said, 'Woman what do you want?'

'Well, now that You ask, Lord,' she answered, 'when You come into Your Kingdom, can my two boys be on Your right hand and on your left?'

And Jesus looked at her and answered very cryptically, 'Are you able to drink from the cup I'm to drink from, and be baptized with the baptism with which I'm about to be baptized?'

Salome must have wondered about such a strange answer to such a simple question, and Jesus probably smiled and said no more. He went into Jerusalem, and you know the story. It wasn't too many days later before the same Salome, with three other women, would be there on a hill right outside the Holy City. They saw Jesus pinned to a cross with two other men — one on His right, one on His left — hanging beside Him the day He entered His Kingdom. And the foolishness of her request must have hit her like a ton of bricks.

What I am asking of the Lord right now can be just as dumb. 'But Lord,' I cry, 'this is a great idea. Bless it, Lord.' And He lovingly says to me, 'You don't know what you're asking. You don't see the whole story. I loved you enough to die on the Cross. Therefore, if I'm not doing what you're begging me to do — what you're naming and claiming — trust Me. And like Salome, in retrospect, you'll be thankful I didn't respond to your request and do your bidding.'

That's the argument Paul makes: Rejoice in tribulation because God fell in love with you and proved His love to you even when you were a sinner; you never have to wonder why the wheel is so dizzying, the pressure so painful, the kiln so hot. And on the basis not of what you feel emotionally nor of what you ascribe to theologically — but because of His love for you unconditionally, you can trust Him to come through totally.

You watch.

You wait.

You'll see.

Heaven Ain't That
Far Away

Who being the brightness of his glory, and the
express image of his person, and upholding all
things by the word of his power, when he had by
himself purged our sins, sat down on the right
hand of the Majesty on high . . .

Hebrews 1:3

AT THE outset of the book of Hebrews, the author tells us why Jesus came, 'consider Jesus' being the central message of the book. In verse 2, he explains that Jesus is God's final Word. Then, in the second half of verse 2 and on into verse 3, we see who He is through seven characteristics of the incomparable Christ. In the text before us, the author continues to consider Jesus . . .

Where He Is

'When he had by himself purged our sins, sat down on the right hand of the Majesty on high . . .' If you were in the sandals of the Hebrew Christians to whom this book was written, this statement would be shocking, even scandalous. Why? Because the priests in the Tabernacle, and later on in the Temple, never sat down. If you went into either place, you would see the brass altar, the huge laver, the table of showbread, the altar of incense, the golden candlestick, the Ark of the Covenant — but not a single chair because the work of a priest was never done.

You see, the sacrifices made by the priests could never take away sin. That's why they had to be offered again and again. Yet this Man, Jesus, the High Priest, sits down. Why? Because, on the Cross, when He cried, IT IS FINISHED, it meant the work was *done*. Thus, when He went into heaven, He sat down; not out of exhaustion, nor out of frustration, but out of complete and total relaxation, knowing the price had been paid for all of Jon Courson's sins — past, present and future.

What He's Doing

'Wherefore he is able also to save them that come unto God by him, seeing he ever liveth to make intercession for them' (Hebrews 7:25). What's our Great High Priest doing? He's talking to the Father about your situation. Think with me about the intercessory ministry of Jesus . . .

Only hours away from His crucifixion, looking at Peter, Jesus said, 'Simon, Satan has desired to sift you like wheat. But I have prayed for you, and when you get through this trial, strengthen the brothers' (Luke 22:31). In other words, 'Satan desires to rip you apart, to wipe you out, to do you in; but I have prayed for you, so when you get through — and you *will* get through — help others.' In Philippians 1:6, the promise is given to us that He who has begun a good work in us will continue to perform it until the end. It's a done deal. Jesus is not pacing. He's sitting in heaven, talking over your situation with the Father with complete confidence that He will see you through ultimately, completely, totally. That's His ministry. . .

There I am, at what used to be Candlestick Park. The Niners are playing the Cowboys. It's a close game. The battle has been brutal. The score has seesawed back and forth. With a time running out in the fourth quarter, the Niners are trailing by six. There's sixty yards to go to score. Steve Young calls the play, sets the team down, takes the snap, drops back. Deep, deep goes Jerry Rice and running alongside him, step for step, is Neon Deion

Sanders. Rice runs a perfect post pattern. He breaks away — but Sanders catches up. The ball is in the air. It's a beautiful pass. Both men go up for it, both have their hands on it. They come down and it looks like Jerry Rice has it — but what's this? We can't believe what we're seeing as a little yellow flag comes out of the hip pocket of the referee. We stand to our feet in anxiety. Who's it against? The referee makes the call against Sanders! The Niners win!

Later on that evening, Tammy and I watch highlights of the game on CNN. I see Steve Young's pass. I see Sanders and Rice both go for it. I see Rice come down, the flag drop — yet I am totally at rest. Why? I know the outcome.

So does our Lord. He knows how it's all going to come out. He promises to see us through. He will complete that which He's begun. That's why He can say, '*When* you make it through, strengthen others . . .'

He's Not Always Seated

Jesus is seated at the right hand of the Father — but He's not *always* seated. Stephen starts preaching about the reality of Jesus Christ. What happens? The crowd becomes so incensed that people start throwing rocks at him. And as the stones begin to strike him, he says, 'I see heaven opening and the Son of God *standing*' (Acts 7:56). I would have thought it would have been just the opposite: I would have thought Jesus would stand as we go through life. Then, when we finally get to heaven, He would say, 'Whew. You made it. I can sit down now.' But, as is true in all areas of spiritual life, Jesus does just the opposite of what I would do. He's sitting down when we're going through life because He's sure we're going to make it. But when we get to heaven, He stands up to welcome us, saying, 'Enter into My joy!'

Here's the challenge for me: I tend to think, 'Well, somewhere way up there beyond the blue, the Lord is sitting at the right hand of the Father, thinking about me, interceding for me. But I suggest to you that nothing could be further from the truth. Think with me . . .

Scientists have been telling us for a number of years that atoms are composed primarily of space. In fact, if I were to squeeze out all the space between the nucleus of the atoms and the electrons, you would be reduced to the size of a speck of dust. That's why scientists say it is theoretically very possible that there could be an entirely different material world in this place right now, which we can't see or hear. Theoretically, if a single atom in Jacksonville were enlarged to the size of a basketball, its electron, proportionately, would be in Philadelphia. There would be ample space for a person, trains, planes, even armies to pass through our midst unnoticed.

What does this have to do with the ministry of Jesus? With Him praying for me? With Him being seated at God's right hand? Everything. You see, Jesus said something radical when He said that the kingdom of God is among you (Luke 17). The word 'among' is translated 'entos' in Greek — a word referring to location. Thus, Jesus said the kingdom of God is not out there beyond the blue. It's among you right here, right now. 'But, Jon,' you protest, 'haven't you always taught that when the Rapture comes, Jesus will come in the clouds?'

He's Always With Us

I suggest we're looking at clouds in the wrong way. Hebrews 12:1 says we are surrounded by a *cloud* of witnesses. Who are these witnesses? Hebrews 11 identifies them as Abraham, Moses, Samson, Gideon, Jephthah — the heroes of faith. So perhaps when Jesus comes, it won't be in a nimbus or a cumulus cloud. It will be, as Jude says, with 10,000 saints in a cloud of witnesses. Where are these witnesses right now? They're not 'out there.' They're right here. Ask Gehazi . . .

'Master, we're in trouble,' he cried. 'The Syrians are surrounding our city. His master, Elisha, a man of miracles, prayed the Lord would open Gehazi's eyes. When He did, Gehazi said, 'Whoa! There are angels everywhere — and they're surrounding the Syrians' (II Kings 6). You see, angels were there all along. It's just that Gehazi was allowed to see a different dimension.

'That's Old Testament,' you say. Turn, then, to 1 Corinthians 11. Paul says, 'when you come together in worship meetings, where gifts are flowing, where the Body is interacting, be careful about certain issues because angels are present in the midst of the congregation.' Why don't we see them? It's because they're in a different dimension. The cloud of witnesses, heroes of faith, and loved ones who have gone ahead of us are not way out there. They're surrounding us. Could it be, then, that when we die or go to be with the Lord, in the event called the Rapture, we don't go somewhere way out there? Could it be that we simply step into the next dimension? Ask Peter, James, and John. Jesus gave them a sneak preview of the coming dimension when, on the Mount of Transfiguration, they suddenly saw Elijah and Moses in their midst. Like Gehazi before them, they were allowed to see into a different dimension; they were made aware of the fact that Elijah and Moses were present, although unseen previously.

If this is true, if heaven's just stepping into a different dimension — and it's right here — what does this mean to me? It means when I pray to my Faithful Friend, my High Priest, Jesus Christ, I'm not saying, 'Hello-o-o. Can You hear me way up there?' No, the Lord is not somewhere way beyond the blue. He is with us always (Matthew 28:20). The kingdom of heaven is among us. The great cloud of witnesses is presently around us. Ministering spirits are in the midst of us. Jesus Himself is in the midst of the congregation. And all of a sudden, I realize heaven ain't that far away — not only because we'll be there soon chronologically, but because the kingdom is surrounding me presently. I don't see it because, like Paul, I see through a glass darkly (I Corinthians 13:12). And, like Gehazi, I can't see what's going on. But I understand there is a dimension of the kingdom round about me. I know with certainty that the Lord is seated at the right hand of the Father, at rest, praying for me.

And I know the same is true for you.

Being Beaten

And the multitude rose up together against them: and the magistrates rent off their clothes, and commanded to beat them. And when they had laid many stripes upon them, they cast them into prison, charging the jailer to keep them safely: who, having received such a charge, thrust them into the inner prison, and made their feet fast in the stocks. And at midnight Paul and Silas prayed, and sang praises unto God: and the prisoners heard them.

Acts 16:22-25

NONE OF us likes to get beat up. I think back a number of years ago to the day when my oldest son came home from kindergarten with tousled hair, torn shirt, and tear-stained cheeks. 'What happened, Peter John?' I asked. With quivering chin, he said, 'The biggest kid in my class beat me up.' I gave Peter a hug and we talked for awhile. The next morning Peter John was up bright and early getting ready for school. As he walked out the door, I couldn't help but notice the baseball bat over his shoulder. 'Where are you going with that bat, Peter?' I asked. With eyes of steel, he said, 'Daddy, today is show and share day. I'm taking my bat to show and share.' Knowing exactly to whom and on whom he wanted to show and share his bat, I insisted he choose something else.

In our text, we see Paul and Silas beaten, bruised, and bloodied — but instead of grabbing their bats and swinging, they glorify God by singing. I suggest three reasons Paul and Silas could sing in such a dark hour . . .

Paul and Silas' beating showed the desperation of the enemy.

When you find yourself beaten up, it means Satan considers you a threat to his dominion of death and darkness. I can recall one such incident that stands out vividly in my memory. It blew my mind when a man, whom I had never met, but who was obviously demonized, looked me in the eye and said, in a voice not completely his own, 'Jon Courson, I know you, and I hate you.' Although it freaked me out initially, I rejoiced later on because whenever Satan and his demons have our number, it means they're threatened.

Paul and Silas' beating was a validation of their ministry.

In Colossians 1:23-24, Paul would later write: 'I Paul am made a minister: who now rejoice in my sufferings for you, and fill up that which is behind of the afflictions of Christ in my flesh for his body's sake, which is the church.' In other words, part of Paul's job as a minister was to fill up — or complete — the sufferings of Jesus.

'Wait a minute,' you say. 'Are you saying that the suffering of Christ on the Cross was not sufficient?' No. His work on the Cross was completely sufficient — validated by His Resurrection. The idea in Colossians relates to the Church. You see, even as Jesus today has thornprints on His brow, nail holes in His hands and feet, lash marks on His back, a spear wound in His side, so, too, His Church must bear the marks of suffering. If His Body is to fully conform to and correctly reflect Him, some, like Paul and Silas, will have to suffer brutally.

Paul and Silas' beating was an indication of their maturity.

You'll never know how far along you are in the maturation process until you are beaten up. Trials neither make us, nor break us. They reveal what is going on inside of us. Thus, when you're beaten up verbally, emotionally, or perhaps even physically, you have an opportunity to see how much the Lord has accomplished in your life. Christians are like tea bags, folks. We'll never know what our flavor is until we're in hot water.

After teaching at a retreat in Palm Springs recently, I decided to go for a walk. It was about 9:30 at night and about 95 degrees outside. Walking briskly down Palm Canyon Drive, I was reading the Word and thinking about this text when, failing to see a puddle in the middle of the pavement, I lost my footing and fell flat on my back. My glasses flew off. My Bible landed in the middle of the street. And I lay there in the mud and blood, rejoicing and thinking what a great illustration it would be for this Sunday. Feeling pretty good as I picked up my Bible and glasses, I continued on. After about three miles of walking and reading, my foot hit a crack in the cement, causing me to lunge forward and break my sandal in the process. Knowing I had to walk back barefoot for five miles on hot cement, I wasn't rejoicing. Thinking one trial per walk should be sufficient, when the second one came my way I was far from singing.

By the time I got back to the hotel, it was 11:30 PM. My feet were cut. I was upset. And then the Lord whispered in my ear, 'You see, Jon, it's not the expected trial which reveals who you are. It's the one that sneaks up behind you which shows what's really going on inside.' We all know of potential trials that will come our way next week — but it's the ones we *don't* expect which will reveal what's going on internally.

You who are beaten up today by persecution on the job, ridicule on the campus, ostracism from your family — Isaiah 54 is for you.

A Future and a Hope

*No weapon that is formed against thee shall
prosper: and every tongue that shall rise against
thee in judgment thou shalt condemn. This is the
heritage of the servants of the Lord, and their
righteousness is of me, saith the Lord.*

Isaiah 54:17

Know this — you who are beaten up — no weapon
which comes against you will prosper. You can be sure of
this. Ask Paul and Silas. Yes, they were beaten up, but
they went out victoriously into deeper ministry and fuller
glory.

Perhaps you're saying, 'It's fine for you spiritual
giants to talk about being beaten up for your spirituality.
Good for you. But that's not where I am. I'm not being
beaten up — I'm being beaten *down* by my family, my
marriage, my job.' You, too, can have hope today because,
although Paul and Silas were beaten up, the jailer was
beaten down — just like you! Roman law decreed that
prison guards were to serve the sentence of any prisoner
who escaped while in their charge. No doubt, in that
Philippian dungeon there were those who had committed
capital offenses, and were about to be executed.
Consequently, this jailer said, 'My head's going to roll
tomorrow, so hand me a sword, and I'll take my life right
now.'

Just as he was about to do himself in, Paul said,
'Don't do that! We're all still here.' So it was that the jailer,
beaten down by circumstances beyond his control, was
saved in the very dungeon in which he sought to take his
own life. If you're beaten down, know this: God is going to
do something wonderful, even in the situation that is
presently depressing or distressing you. If you're beaten

up, like Paul and Silas, God will work *through* you to bring others to Himself. If you're beaten down, like the Philippian jailer, God will work *for* you to bring you to Himself. Whether you're beaten up or beaten down, you can rejoice. Why? Because Satan has been beaten back. Turn to Isaiah 53 . . .

> *Surely he hath borne our griefs, and carried our sorrows: yet we did esteem him stricken, smitten of God, and afflicted. But he was wounded for our transgression, he was bruised for our iniquities: the chastisement of our peace was upon him; and with his stripes we are healed. All we like sheep have gone astray; we have turned every one to his own way; and the Lord hath laid on him the iniquity of us all.*
>
> Isaiah 53:4-6

Satan has been beaten back because the back of Jesus was beaten. By Whom? By the Father (Isaiah 53:6). The Father beat the Son. Why? One reason: to purchase a bride for Him. The Father said, 'I love My Son so much I'm going to smite Him, beat Him, and lay upon Him the judgment, wrath, and damnation which should have fallen on Jon — because forgiven, pure, and robed in righteousness, Jon will make a perfect bride for Him.'

Now, if that be so — if God the Father paid that kind of price for me to be the bride of His Son, if He beat His Son in order that I might be healed — then He is equally committed to continue to do good things through me and good things for me.

You who are beaten down today by a relationship which isn't working out, by money which isn't coming in, by a job which isn't opening up — Isaiah 54 is for you . . .

Sing, O barren, thou that didst not bear; break
forth into singing and cry aloud, thou that didst
not travail with child: for more are the children of
the desolate than the children of the married wife,
saith the Lord

Isaiah 54:1

Sing! Shout for joy, you who are barren and dry,
you who are beaten down by the circumstances of life;
because you will be more fruitful, more prosperous, more
blessed than the one who seems to be doing so well right
now.

Enlarge the place of thy tent, and let them stretch
forth the curtains of thine habitations: spare not,
lengthen thy cords, and strengthen thy stakes:
For thou shalt break forth on the right hand and
on the left; and thy seed shall inherit the Gentiles,
and make the desolate cities to be inhabited.

Isaiah 54:2-3

What are you to do, you who are beaten down?
Because His back was beaten, know this: He's going to do
good things for you. Don't kill yourself. Don't curse. Don't
mourn. Don't gripe. Don't despair. Rather, sing out today
and say, 'Lord, if You loved me enough to smite Your Son
for me, I trust You. And even though I feel barren, dry,
and desolate, I am going to enlarge my tent and prepare
for Your blessing.'

And do you know what will happen as a result?
The world around you — your fellow prisoners — will be
drawn to Jesus. How do I know? Look again at the next
three verses following our text:

And suddenly there was a great earthquake, so
that the foundations of the prison were shaken:
and immediately all the doors were opened, and

every one's bands were loosed. And the keeper of the prison awaking out of his sleep, and seeing the prison doors open, he drew out his sword, and would have killed himself, supposing that the prisoners had been fled. But Paul cried with a loud voice, saying, Do thyself no harm: for we are all here.

Acts 16:26-28

'For we are *all* here . . .' This is amazing. I mean, why didn't these prisoners run for their lives the moment their prison doors were opened? The answer can only be that these hardened criminals were more intrigued by what they saw in Paul and Silas than by the thought of escape. They were hungrier for freedom in their souls than freedom from their cells.

Dear saint, please understand that the purpose of praise and worship is not so that we may escape *from* our situation. The purpose of praise and worship is to bring God *into* our situation. For then those around us can see that regardless of whether we are beaten up or beaten down, Satan has been beaten back — through the beaten back of the Son.

Weeping or Whining?

Mine eye trickleth down, and ceaseth not, without any intermission, Till the Lord look down, and behold from heaven. Mine eye affecteth mine heart because of all the daughters of my city.

Lamentations 3:49-51

I HAD a very interesting evening last Wednesday. After teaching the first three chapters of Lamentations, I went home, talked awhile with my wife, Tammy, and then crashed. At 11:30 PM, I shot up in bed wide-awake with my mind in overdrive and my heart stirred.

Knowing the Lord was speaking to me, I got up, grabbed a notebook and pen, and began to write. When I finished, I glanced at the clock and it was 4:30 AM. I don't say this to impress you with my spirituality — for most of the time, I snooze right through such incidents. I say it to impress upon you my belief that this is the Word of the Lord for you and me today.

Consider, as I did in those early morning hours, the prophets, Jonah and Jeremiah . . .

Both Jonah and Jeremiah Hesitated
When Called to the Ministry

Jonah hesitated out of hostility. Called to minister to the most vicious and sadistic people in the history of the world, Jonah wanted to see God blast the Ninevites, not bless them. He wanted them to experience God's fury, not His forgiveness. Jeremiah hesitated out of insecurity. Feeling incapable of carrying out the Lord's mission for him, Jeremiah protested, 'Oh, Lord, God. I cannot speak. I am but a child (Jeremiah 1:6). I can't do this, Lord. I'm not ready to be a prophet.'

What about us? Jesus said, 'You shall be My witnesses in Jerusalem and Judea and Samaria and to the uttermost parts of the earth' (Acts 1:8). And, perhaps like Jeremiah, we hesitate because of our insecurity. 'Oh, Lord, I can't do that,' we argue. 'I don't know enough Bible verses. I haven't had enough experience. That's not my personality.' Gang, God will never ask you to do that which He does not empower you to do. Jesus didn't say, 'You *should* be My witnesses' or 'You *better* be My witnesses.' He said, 'You *shall* be My witnesses.' It *will* happen.

Both Jonah and Jeremiah Were Sent into a City

Jonah was sent to Nineveh — headquarters of the powerful Assyrian Empire, political capital of the world. But it was almost impossible to get Jonah *into* Nineveh. In fact, he never would have made it there without a storm at sea and a whale for an escort. Jeremiah was sent to Jerusalem — the city of God, the spiritual capital of the world. But it was almost impossible to get Jeremiah *out* of Jerusalem.

Before the Babylonians destroyed Jerusalem, King Nebuchadnezzar sent an emissary to Jeremiah, saying, 'We know you're a prophet of God. Therefore, we'll take care of you wherever you choose to go throughout the entire Empire.' Jeremiah's response? 'Thanks, but no thanks. I'm going to stay here with my people' (Jeremiah 40:4-6).

Both Jonah and Jeremiah Were Separated From Their Friends and Families

Jonah was physically separated from friends and family by hundreds of miles geographically. Jeremiah was separated from friends and family emotionally when his friends forsook him and his brothers dealt treacherously with him (Jeremiah 11, 12).

Both Jonah and Jeremiah Were Manhandled

After learning Jonah was the reason for the storm which threatened their lives, his fellow sailors reluctantly threw him overboard. The priests and prophets of Jerusalem, who cast Jeremiah into dungeons on five separate occasions, manhandled him not reluctantly but readily.

Both Jonah and Jeremiah Were Cast into a Pit

Jonah referred to his accommodations in the belly of the whale as the pit of hell itself (Jonah 2:2). Jeremiah was cast into a pit which, because it had previously been a holding tank for water, was filled with mud and mire. Like Jonah, Jeremiah knew if he kept sinking, he would soon die (Jeremiah 38:6).

Both Jonah and Jeremiah Cried Out to the Lord

Jonah was delivered by the command of God when he was deposited on the beach by the great fish. Jeremiah was delivered by the hand of man when Ebedmelech had compassion on him and pulled him out of the pit (Jeremiah 38:13).

Both Jonah and Jeremiah Preached to the People

Jonah preached a single sentence: 'In forty days, Nineveh will be destroyed.' He offered no solution, gave no instruction, showed no compassion. Jeremiah preached a multitude of messages, not for forty days, but for forty years. With illustration, persuasion, and passion, Jeremiah poured out his heart to the people of Jerusalem.

Both Jonah and Jeremiah Saw the Peoples' Response to God

Through his single-sentence-sermon, Jonah witnessed a revival from God when the entire city of Nineveh turned to the Lord in humility and repentance. After preaching forty years, Jeremiah witnessed the rejection of God when not one single person was saved.

Let this be a word to every one of us in ministry today. For forty years, this prophet — esteemed by heaven and studied by Christians throughout the ages — saw not one conversion. Yet if Jonah and Jeremiah were ministering today, whom would the books be written about? Whom would the photographers photograph, and the interviewers question? Whom would be on the cover of *Christianity Today*? Jonah.

What about Jeremiah? He'd be sitting in the back row of one of Jonah's 'Effective Ministry Seminars,' taking notes and trying to figure out what he'd done wrong. Dear people, the greatest revival that ever happened took place through a man whose heart was not right with God. Therefore, we are, oh, so foolish if we evaluate ministry numerically. I don't care how much fruit you see in your ministry, how much approval you get, how many folks come forward, or how many souls you've led to the Lord.

Don't evaluate ministry on the basis of whom God uses. After all, God used a donkey to talk to Balaam, and a heathen Pharaoh to speak to a godly Josiah.

Jesus taught that the first shall be last and the last first. This means that in heaven there will be all kinds of surprises when the Lord says to the Jonahs, who are sitting in the front row waiting for their rewards, 'Why don't you move back a few thousand rows because, although I used you, your heart was far from Me.' And to the Jeremiahs — to those who were thought to be total failures, to those whose ministry never seemed to 'come together,' to those who looked like losers in the eyes of men — 'Well done, good and faithful servant. Come! Enter into the joy of the Lord.'

That's why Paul says we're not to judge anything before that time (I Corinthians 4:5). We're not to evaluate whom is successful and whom is not because only the Lord knows the heart of man.

Both Jonah and Jeremiah Sat on a Hillside at the End of Their Ministries

Jonah whined about his possession — a gourd that had been destroyed by a worm. Jeremiah wept for the people who had rejected him, imprisoned him, beat him, mocked and ignored him. This absolutely astounds me. I mean, if I were Jeremiah, I know it would have been my tendency to say, 'For forty years, I warned you. And what did you do? You threw me in prison, gave me forty lashes, and turned your back on me. Now it's your turn to get beat up a bit.' But Jeremiah didn't do that. He sat on a hillside with hot tears running down his dusty cheeks.

What about us? Do we whine — Or do we weep? Do we whine about how we're going to make our house payment, about why no one appreciates us, about why we don't feel good? Or do we weep for those in Medford who walk in darkness, for those in Grants Pass who don't know God, for those in Jacksonville who are going to hell?

If your tears were measured over the last five years, how many would have been shed for the unsaved? On what do our prayers center? 'Bless *my* ministry. Bless *my* family. Bless *my* friends,' or 'God have mercy upon those who don't know You, who are down on You, who are going to be destroyed ultimately unless they turn to You?' Folks, we will become shrimpy, shrunken, little people if all we are concerned about is *our* little world. The Lord desires us to be big people — expansive in our view of *His* world.

In the darkness of those early morning hours, I brokenly said, 'Lord, I'm much more like Jonah than Jeremiah. I whine more about my gourds than about Your people. But Father, what made Jeremiah, Jeremiah? What gave him the ability to hang in there for forty years with people who rejected him, abused him, despised him? Where did he get that kind of compassion? How does a Jonah like me become a Jeremiah for You?

As I searched through the Books of Jeremiah and Lamentations, I found nothing. Oh, sure, I could speculate that it was the work of the Holy Spirit upon him, or the result of prayer within him, but I needed more than speculation. The next day I wrestled and struggled and discussed the question to no avail. 'Perhaps there is no conclusion, no summation,' I reasoned. But in my heart, I knew the way of the Lord is not to leave us in that kind of frustration.

And then the Lord led me to Luke for the solution to this situation, for there we see not Jonah, not Jeremiah — but Jesus. And in Jesus *all* answers are *always* found. He is the Solution to *every* problem, the Explanation to *every* dilemma.

> *And when he was come near, he beheld the city, and wept over it . . .*
>
> *Luke 19:41*

As Jesus was about to enter Jerusalem to die for the sins of humanity, knowing Jerusalem was headed for another wave of persecution, He stopped on a hillside and wept for the city — just as Jeremiah had done. Jesus showed the same compassion Jeremiah had shown, the same broken heart, the same tear-filled eyes. That is why when asked who people thought Jesus was, His disciples answered that some thought He was Jeremiah back from the dead (Matthew 16:14). Interestingly, not one person mistook Jesus for Jonah.

The only way I will have compassion for Jacksonville, Grants Pass, Medford, or for colleagues, friends, and neighbors is if Jesus Christ weeps for them through me. What does this mean? It means that if I spend increased amounts of time with Jesus, I will become more like Him. I'll see what He sees, and feel what He feels.

In 1 Samuel 22, a rag-tag group of losers and renegades, who were in debt, distressed, and discontent, gathered around David. And as they hung around their leader, who was together and sharp and effective, they became like him. So, too, as we spend more and more time with our Leader, we, who are in debt, distressed, and discontented, will become more like Him, feeling what He does, and seeing people the way He sees them. As we spend time with Him, whining will cease and weeping will increase. Why? Because, although we choose not to think about our next-door neighbor going to hell, Jesus sees him eternally headed for damnation — and His heart breaks. While we believe in hell theologically, Jesus knows about hell experientially. That is why He spoke more about hell than about heaven. Forty years before the destruction of Jerusalem, Jesus wept over the city, knowing what was to happen. And in these last moments before the destruction of the world, He weeps again.

Precious people, you'll know how close you are to the Lord at any given moment by what you're crying about. Are you whining for yourself, or weeping for the lost? May the Father in His great mercy change us Jonahs into Jeremiahs as we spend time with Jesus. May He turn our whining to weeping, our self-pity to compassion, and our hardened hearts to tear-stained cheeks.

In Jesus' name.

Enduring Tribulation

But he that shall endure unto the end, the same shall be saved.

Matthew 24:13

MATTHEW 24:13 is not only applicable prophetically, but also presently; for in this world, Jesus said we
would have tribulations. Our Christian life is a race to be
run (Hebrews 12:1), and our race, dear people, is not a
100-meter sprint. It's a marathon.

'But he that shall endure unto the end, the same
shall be saved.' The word 'saved' is translated 'sozo' in
Greek. It's a word which refers to the full orb of God's
blessing. In other words, according to Matthew 24:13, you
who endure the marathon will experience the sozo, the
blessing of God upon yourself, your family, your walk with
the Lord, your ministry, your finances, and your vocation.
You will experience the full orb of God's blessing in every
area of your life.

The Call to Endurance

In the fifth chapter of his book, James picks up on
this theme of enduring until the end . . .

> Behold, we count them happy which endure. Ye
> have heard of the patience of Job, and have seen
> the end of the Lord; that the Lord is very pitiful
> [compassionate], and of tender mercy.
>
> James 5:11

This passage brings a question to our minds: 'Lord,
if You are merciful and compassionate, then why do You

allow troubles to come against us and problems to plague us? Why don't You do something, Lord?'

According to James, the answer lies in remembering the heroes of the Old Testament . . .

There was one prophet who felt exceedingly weary. His name was Jeremiah. Jeremiah's problems were mounting on all sides, and he was about to throw in the towel as far as ministry was concerned. Listen to what the Lord said to him: 'Jeremiah, you have run against the footmen and if you faint in running against the footmen, how will you run against the horses? You've been engaged in some battles and some tribulation, but if you're fainting in these present days, in these present battles, what are you going to do when the horses come, when the big problems hit you?' (Jeremiah 12:5).

The Lord went on to tell him that the Babylonians were coming to carry the Jews out of their homeland. 'You think it's tough now, Jeremiah, but I see what's coming. I am preparing you by allowing you to go through these difficulties and trials. I'm preparing you, son, like a coach who trains a runner. I'm allowing you to go through hard times to prepare you for what I know lies ahead.'

'Well, then,' we wonder, 'if God used hard times to prepare Jeremiah for the Babylonians, why didn't He save Himself and Jeremiah a lot of trouble and just destroy the Babylonians in the first place?' For the same reason He doesn't destroy the problems in our lives: because this world has rejected His rule. Ever since the Garden of Eden, mankind has thumbed his nose at God and demanded liberation, saying, 'We'll do what we want.' And our loving Father says to His children, to this planet, 'OK, have it your way.'

Because all of humanity throughout all of history has rebelled against God, we have disease and death, pollution and war, troubles and problems. Not only in the world generally, but in our worlds personally — whenever you and I rebel against the way of God, we reap devastation, destruction and sadness. The Father does not promise to keep us from problems, but to be with us *in* them. Since He sees what is coming two years down the road, He says, 'I see what's ahead, and I'm going to work with you right now to get you ready. I'm going to have you race against the footmen, so that when the horses come stampeding through, you'll be able to endure.'

I think of Mama giraffe. Did you know that when she gives birth, she does so from a standing position? This means when Baby giraffe is born, he immediately falls on his head ten feet to the ground. Mama then does something which absolutely intrigues me. After quickly stretching her neck down to check Baby's condition, she will stand upright once again, swing her front leg, and kick him. Baby then tries to stand up, wobbles, and falls to the ground in exhaustion. No sooner does Baby collapse, than Mama winds up her leg and kicks him once more. This happens three, four, or five times until Baby finally musters up enough strength — the adrenaline flowing, terror filling his heart — to stand up.

Once Baby gets up on all fours, Mama again swings her leg and kicks his legs out from under him. And the process is repeated two, three, or four more times. The result? Within the first hour of his birth, Baby learns how to get up quickly and to move away from Mama readily.

Why does Mama giraffe do this? Because she instinctively understands that watching the birth of her baby were leopards, lions, hyenas and jackals. Since giraffes are defenseless if they cannot move in a pack, Baby must learn quickly how to stand up and get moving — even if it means getting mad at Mama and not understanding what she's doing.

Maybe you can relate. 'What are you doing, God? I just barely get up and BAM, I'm down again. I just get going and BOOM, I'm flat on my face once more. What's happening?' The Lord is teaching you something. He loves you and me enough that — even though we misunderstand Him, shake our fist at Him, or turn our back on Him — He says, 'I know this is needed in your life in order that you might stand and be established, that you might be able to run with the horses, that you might endure.'

The Key to Endurance

By faith Moses, when he was come to years, refused to be called the son of Pharaoh's daughter; choosing rather to suffer affliction with the people of God, than to enjoy the pleasures of sin for a season; esteeming the reproach of Christ greater than the treasures in Egypt.

Hebrews 11:24-26

When Moses was forty years old, having grown up in Pharaoh's court, he was in line to ascend the very throne of Pharaoh; yet he chose instead to take on the reproach of Christ, for it was a greater treasure than the best Egypt had to offer. I like that! Sure, we go through sufferings and reproaches, tribulations and difficulties, but even they are better than the best the world has to offer us with its heartache and disappointment and disillusionment.

At forty years of age, Moses came to this conclusion. 'I would rather be with God's people and suffer than remain in this place where the pleasures of sin are for but a season.' And he split the scene. Then he began to lead God's people out of Egypt. For forty years, he led them through the wilderness. It wasn't easy. It was hot and dry. You think you're going through dry times? Think of Moses! You think people don't like you? Scripture says three million Jews rose up, with rocks in hand, ready to stone him.

How did Moses make it? How did he endure the rejection, the dry times, the constant troubles from within and without? Look at verse 27: 'By faith he forsook Egypt, not fearing the wrath of the king: for he endured as seeing him who is invisible.'

That's the key. Moses endured seeing Him who is invisible. In other words, he saw God's hand in everything and in every situation.

Two days ago, I talked with a lady who was devastated. She was ready to leave everything to marry a man who lived across the country. Although she hadn't known him very long, she felt it was providential. But the day before she was to leave, she discovered some things about him that indicated he had some serious problems. She had packed her goods, cut all her ties, and sold her business — only to find out a day before the wedding that it wasn't going to happen. I understood her feeling of disappointment as she wondered, 'What's the Lord doing? Where is He? Why is He allowing this to happen to me?'

In response, I told her it would be as if I had come home and walked in to see my daughter, Christy, unwrapping a king-size Snickers bar. As she was just about to take a big bite, I lunged at her, grabbed the Snickers from her, and threw it to the floor, saying, 'Christy, haven't you heard the news? It has just been discovered that every Snickers in Oregon has been laced with arsenic. One bite will kill you!' Now, at that point, Christy could either say, 'Oh, Dad, I was just ready to enjoy that Snickers bar and you took it from me. How mean!' Or she could say, 'Oh, Daddy, thanks for rescuing me! You knew something I didn't. You saved my life!'

So, too, when the Father intervened in that lady's situation, she had a choice to make. She could say, 'Why is this happening to me?' Or, she could see Him who is invisible, see His hand in everything, and say, 'Father, thank You for grabbing the Snickers from me. You caught me just in time!'

Dear saint, you have a choice to make right now in whatever you're going through. You can either shrivel up, pull in, fall down, and fade away like the shallow seed in Mark 4; or you can endure, seeing Him who is invisible, seeing His hand in everything and everything in His hand. Look at His hand, and do you know what you will see? A nailprint. The invisible God became a visible Man in Christ Jesus. As I see His nail-scarred hand, I have no choice but to say, 'If You loved me enough to be pinned to the Cross for me, to be plunged into hell for me, I will trust You by faith — even though I may not understand.'

What is faith? According to Hebrews 11, it is the substance of things hoped for, the evidence of things not seen. There is no such thing as 'blind faith.' On the contrary, faith sees more than unbelief ever will because it sees into an entirely different dimension. 'Through faith we understand that the worlds were framed by the Word of God, so that things which are seen were not made of things which do appear' (Hebrews 11:3).

The Hebrew word for *create* is 'bara,' which means 'to make something out of that which does not previously exist.' In other words, God made everything from nothing. It wasn't that He re-fashioned material; but rather, by faith, He spoke the worlds into existence. So, too, the world in which you personally live — your children, your job, your ministry, your marriage, your finances — is presently being framed. You are framing your world, even as God framed this world by speaking the Word.

Think of a carpenter framing a house. The house is formed by how it's framed. Maybe you have framed your world with unbelief and griping, complaining and doubting, saying, 'Why me? How come? Where's God?' Maybe you don't like the house you live in because the walls are falling down, the tiles are falling off, and it's a miserable place to live. Don't blame God. *You* built it. *You* framed it with complaints and cynicism.

We have another option. We can say, 'By faith I will frame my world with the Word of God. I will study the Scriptures. I will claim the promises and believe them by faith: All things work together for good to them that love God, to them who are called according to His purpose (Romans 8:28). The joy of the Lord is my strength (Nehemiah 8:10). For in Him I live and move and have my being (Acts 17:28). But my God shall supply all my need according to His riches in glory by Christ Jesus (Philippians 4:8).'

Today I can build a house by trusting God, by seeing Him who is invisible, and believing Him for the promises — or I can murmur to my wife when I get home. God judged the nation of Israel because they murmured in their tents (Deuteronomy 1:27). Husbands and wives got together and spoke words of complaint and unbelief to each other, and a great plague struck the land. Speak the promises of God to each other. Go on record. Build a world that is in accordance with the Word of God as revealed in Scripture. Speak words of faith, and you'll endure.

Winston Churchill, 248 lbs. of solid inspiration, single-handedly saved England in the days of the Blitzkrieg. Night after night, the third Reich flew planes over London, unloading thousands of bombs. Hitler felt, as did other international observers, that England would fall easily. But this bulldog of a man, Winston Churchill, went on the air, time and time again, calling his nation to hang on, to believe. And England didn't go down. Years later, one of his alma maters, an exclusive prep school, asked him to speak at graduation. He accepted the invitation. The headmaster of the school was elated. For weeks he told the student body, 'Soon Winston Churchill is coming. The most powerful orator in history is going to speak here. When he comes, bring your pencils and paper and take note of every word he says.'

Finally the day came. The graduation service began. The students sitting behind the speakers' podium had pencils and paper poised. The parents and guests settled in for a long, inspirational speech. After many flowery introductions, Churchill finally arose from his chair, took the podium, and turned around to address the young men behind him. 'Gentlemen,' he said, 'Never give up. Never give up. Never, never, never, never, never, never, never!' Then he sat down. The students were stunned. The audience was amazed. And none of them ever, ever, ever forgot it.

That's what Jesus says to us. 'Never give up. He that endures to the end shall be saved.' So, when the Father seems to be kicking your wobbly legs out from under you, when you seem to be running hard against the footmen, know this: It's all working for your ultimate salvation.

Endure, gang, by seeing the invisible.

Endure by framing your world with faith.

And never give up.

Prickly Problems

And lest I should be exalted above measure through the abundance of the revelations, there was given to me a thorn in the flesh, the messenger of Satan to buffet me, lest I should be exalted above measure. For this thing I besought the Lord thrice, that it might depart from me.

II Corinthians 12:7-9

IT'S A most prickly problem, a truly thorny issue, which we hear about regularly and with which we struggle frequently: Why does the pain persist? Why does the problem keep poking me? I've prayed about it, claimed victory over it, and want deliverance from it. But it just seems to always be there, causing consternation and agitation within me. Why does the problem remain?

If you have wrestled with such issues, the text before us is just for you. What was the thorn in Paul's flesh? Some think it was a demon hassling him. Some say it was a person who was harassing him. Others believe it was a physical problem. Some suggest Paul suffered from the recurring migraines associated with certain types of malaria. Others surmise Paul had an eye disease due to the fact that the Galatians were willing to give him their own eyes, if that were possible (Galatians 4:15) — implying Paul's were impaired.

According to a second-century document, Paul squinted constantly and his eyes ran continually. 'You see with what large letters I write to you . . .' Paul writes in Galatians 6:11 — the implication being, 'I don't see so well.' Although we don't know for certain what Paul's thorn in the flesh was, this much we do know: it wasn't a sliver because the Greek word used for 'thorn' is the same used for 'tent stake.'

The Bedouins are a nomadic people who, with the exception of the TV antennas sticking out of their tents, live today as they have lived for thousands of years. Since their only concession to modern society is color TV, the 'thorn' we read of here in II Corinthians would be similar to the 18-inch spikes used by the Bedouins to pitch their tents today — and the spike used by Jael in Judges 4, with which she nailed Sisera, her enemy, to the ground. Why did God allow this tent stake, this problem, this pain in Paul's life? Our text gives three reasons . . .

To Produce Protection

In the verses prior to our text, Paul explained to the Corinthian believers how he had been caught up into heaven (II Corinthians 12:1-4). Therefore, because he had such an incredible, unspeakable experience, the thorn in his flesh kept him from becoming proud.

One morning, during a particularly successful season for Speedy Morris, head basketball coach at LaSalle University, his wife knocked on the bathroom door as he was shaving.

'Speedy, honey, someone from *Sports Illustrated* is on the phone.'

'*Sports Illustrated!*' thought Speedy. With lather still on his face, he grabbed a towel and stumbled down the stairs.

'Sports Illustrated?' he said eagerly, adjusting the phone to his ear.

'Yes,' said a cheerful voice on the other end. 'For 75 cents an issue, you can subscribe to *Sports Illustrated* for a full year!'

And Speedy's bubble was burst.

Knowing you and me, the Lord point blank says, 'Pride goes before destruction and a haughty spirit before a fall' (Proverbs 16:18). Therefore, to protect us, He sends pains and problems to hedge us in. Through the harlot Gomer as a picture of Israel, and the prophet Hosea a picture of the everlasting love of God, God says,

> *Therefore, behold, I will hedge up thy way with thorns, and make a wall, that she shall not find her paths. And she shall follow after her lovers, but she shall not overtake them; and she shall seek them, but shall not find them. Then shall she say, I will go and return to my first husband, for then was it better with me than now.*
>
> *Hosea 2:6-7*

The Lord knows my vulnerabilities. And He knows your weaknesses. Thus, by His grace, the thorns He allows in us are truly His protection for us.

To Propel Prayer

I have found oftentimes when my prayer life becomes lax or lazy, I find myself estranged from my Father. But prickly problems indeed propel me to pray. So, too, as one who prayed night and day, Paul, nonetheless, prayed three times for the thorn in his flesh to be removed (II Timothy 1:3, I Thessalonians 2:13, Romans 1:9, I Thessalonians 5:17).

When you are dealing with an issue, which returns again and again, what should you do? Pray and pray and pray until you are either healed, delivered, set free — or until the Lord speaks into your heart the reason why the problem will remain. Pray for either a release from the thorn or a revelation concerning the situation. Such is the model of Paul, and of Jesus.

Three times in the Garden of Gethsemane Jesus prayed, 'Father if it be possible, let this cup pass from Me' (Matthew 17:39, 42, 44). Because of us, the thorn of the Cross was not removed, but Jesus received peace when He concluded His prayer, 'Thy will be done.' Keep praying, saint. The Lord will either remove your thorn, your pain, your struggle — or He will give you understanding to go along with it.

To Precede Power

It was after Paul prayed three times for deliverance that at last he could say, 'Most gladly, therefore will I rather glory in my infirmities, that the power of Christ may rest upon me' (verse 9).

'Let me mow the lawn,' begged Benjamin. 'OK,' I said. So, grabbing hold of the handles to my push mower, Ben pushed and grunted as the veins stuck out on his four-year-old neck.

'Help me, Daddy!' he called.

'OK, Ben,' I said. And with Ben in my arms, mowed a few strips of the lawn.

When we decided to take a break, it was an excited and elated Benny who ran in the house yelling, 'Mommy! Mommy! I mowed the lawn!'

What does God want to do? He wants to empower your life. But it's not until you come to the end of your rope that you can see your need for His strength. That's why the strongest people you will ever meet are those, who at some point in their lives, have absorbed a 'thorn in the flesh' and have come to be at peace with it.

Rapport with Me

Whenever I think I am the only one suffering from a particular thorn in my flesh, the judgment hall of Pilate tells me otherwise. You see, it was there that Jesus absorbed not a single thorn in His flesh, but an entire crown of thorns, pressed into His skull (Mark 15:17). Therefore, He can relate to whatever problem I face; whatever battle I fight; whatever sharp, pointed thorn I endure because He has been there, tempted in all points like me — yet without sin (Hebrews 4:15).

Reminder to Me

My tendency is to say, 'Only my thorn is heavy.' But the crown of thorns on Jesus' brow reminds me that because of Adam's sin, we're *all* cursed with thorns (Genesis 3:18). Therefore, God is not picking on me alone. We're all in this together, for every one of us will bear our own thorn.

Revival within Me

The crown of thorns preceded the Cross of Calvary, which opened the way to heaven for me — where there will be no more tears, no more pain, no more thorns. This produces revival within my heart, and renewed love for the One who absorbed more thorns than I could ever imagine.

Precious sisters, dear brother, don't try to remove the thorn the Lord has given you. Embrace it and see it produce protection in your walk, prayer in your heart, power in your life — all to the glory of the One who endured the thorns; all to the praise of the One who paid the price.

A Word to the Weary

Come unto me, all ye that labour and are heavy laden, and I will give you rest. Take my yoke upon you, and learn of me; for I am meek and lowly in heart: and ye shall find rest unto your souls. For my yoke is easy, and my burden is light.

Matthew 11:28-30

IT REMAINS one of the most mystifying missing-person cases in FBI files. The date was August 15, 1930. On that day, a 45-year-old New York State Supreme Court Justice named Joseph Crater, after spending an evening eating out with friends, hailed a taxi and was never seen or heard from again. The FBI immediately became involved, and suspected a kidnapping by someone who held a judicial grudge against Justice Crater. But that didn't seem to pan out. Then they suspected Mafia activity because Justice Crater was an enemy of the Mafia. But, again, that led nowhere.

There is only one clue which remains to this day. When Mrs. Crater returned to their apartment the evening her husband disappeared, there on the table was a large check made out to her and a note attached to the check in her husband's handwriting, which simply said, 'I am very, very tired. Love, Joe.'

The question remains: Were Judge Crater's words nothing more than a comment at the end of a particularly trying day?

Or was his note saying, 'I'm tired; I'm fatigued; I'm weary. I give up?'

To this day we can't be sure. For lack of further evidence, it is presently believed Judge Joseph Crater took a taxi to an unknown destination, where he took his own life because weariness had weighted his soul. I think all of us, from time to time, can relate to that kind of weariness. I think all of us feel deep fatigue occasionally. I'm not speaking of physical fatigue, the kind of fatigue you feel after mowing the lawn or playing a set of tennis. No, I'm speaking of the weariness which comes from life itself . . .

If you are of average weight and height, here is what you will go through in an average 24-hour period: Your heart will beat 103,689 times. Your blood will travel 168 million miles, as your heart pumps approximately 4 ounces per beat. You will breathe 23,040 times, inhaling 438 cubic feet of air. Your stomach will take in 3.5 pounds of food and 2.9 quarts of liquid. You will lose 7-8 pounds of waste. If you are a man, you will speak 4,800 words. If you are a woman, you will speak close to 7,000 words. You will move 750 muscles, and exercise 7 million brain cells. No wonder we're tired! But there is weariness much more draining than physical fatigue. It's the kind of weariness you feel when you just don't know if you can go on another day.

It's the weariness a father feels when his child is doing wrong. It's the weariness a friend feels who has been abandoned or misunderstood. It's the weariness a wife feels whose husband has rejected her. It's the weariness which can take a toll on even the most seemingly successful individual, even on a Joseph Crater.

Come unto Me . . .

There is One, however, in the history of humanity, who came and declared this word: 'Come to Me, all ye that are weary.' How I appreciate that! The Lord of the universe invited anyone who is weary to come to Him. If I were the Lord, I don't know if I would make that kind of invitation. Keep in mind at this point in Matthew's Gospel, we see Israel rejecting His invitation to make Him King.

Consequently, no longer is Jesus speaking to a nation corporately, saying, 'Repent. The kingdom of heaven is at hand.' Instead, He is speaking to individuals personally, saying, 'Come to Me, any who are weary, any who are laboring.'

Would you have called this group of people? I'm not sure I would. If I were giving an invitation, I don't think I would have said, 'Come unto me all you who are laboring and feeling weary as though you're depressed to the point of death, despairing because of divorce or disease, death or discouragement.'

No, I think I would say, 'Come unto me, all you who are happy. Let's celebrate life together! Let's lift each other's spirits! Or maybe I would have said, 'Come unto me, all you who are wealthy. Come and share your prosperity! Or maybe 'Come unto me all you who are wise. Let's dialogue and philosophize and interact intellectually.'

The personal invitation Jesus extended to people individually as the nation corporately rebelled against Him was: Anyone who is weary come to Me. Those are My people — the weary ones.

Come unto Me . . .

Jesus didn't say, 'Run to Me.' So often in my weariness, I can't run. I can only stumble to Him, or crawl before Him. But that's OK. He just said, '*Come,*' any way we can.

A Future and a Hope

Come unto *Me* . . .

He didn't say, 'Go to church.'

He didn't say, 'Listen to a sermon.'

He didn't say, 'Get some counseling.'

He didn't say, 'Read a book.'

He said, 'Come to *Me*.'

All Ye That Labour . . .

What causes us to be weary in our labor? Turn to Exodus 5. The people of Israel were down in Egypt. 400 years previously, they left the Land of Promise due to famine, and headed south to Egypt, where there was plenty to eat. They lived there for awhile, enjoying the abundance and prosperity. But suddenly the situation changed when a new Pharaoh came on the scene, looked at the Jewish people and said, 'We must control these people. How? We'll enslave them.'

So, for hundreds of years, the people of God were enslaved by the Egyptians, baking bricks in the blistering, burning sun for the construction of Pharaoh's monuments. It has been documented that the Israelites baked enough bricks to build a wall ten feet high and five feet thick, from LA to New York City. That's a lot of bricks! When Moses said, 'Let my people go,' Pharaoh answered:

> *Ye shall no more give the people straw to make brick, as heretofore; let them go and gather straw for themselves. And the tale of the bricks, which they did make heretofore, ye shall lay upon them: ye shall not diminish ought thereof: for they be idle; therefore they cry, saying, Let us go and sacrifice to our God. Let there more work be laid*

upon the men, that they may labour therein; and
let them not regard vain words.

Exodus 5:7-9

The word 'labour' used in verse 9 is the same as the word 'labour' Jesus used in Matthew 11: 'Come unto Me all ye that labour . . .' Do you sometimes feel like you're stuck in Egypt — endlessly making bricks for Pharaoh under the blistering sun? Maybe you said, 'I'm going to Egypt. I'm going to labor to get ahead in my career,' or, 'I'm going to work hard for this material thing.' And for awhile, it seemed enjoyable — but then, just like Pharaoh, it turned against you, and the very thing you thought would be wonderful is now a taskmaster, cracking the whip and enslaving you.

'Come to Me,' the Lord says. 'All you who are weary from labor; all you who have realized Pharaoh is a fake and Egypt is a rip-off, come to Me.' We have a tendency to think, 'I'm going to be so happy when I accomplish this task, when I reach that goal, when I get this business, or that toy.' And we labor and labor until we finally say, 'This isn't working out the way I thought it could, the way the commercials promised it would. I'm miserable. I'm tired. I'm weary.' Jesus says, 'Come to Me, all ye that labour.'

And Are Heavy-Laden . . .

What does it mean to be heavy-laden? Turn to Isaiah 1 . . .

Ah sinful nation, a people laden with iniquity, a
seed of evildoers, children that are corrupters:
they have forsaken the Lord, they have provoked
the Holy One of Israel unto anger, they are gone
away backward. Why should ye be stricken any
more? Ye will revolt more and more: the whole

head is sick, and the whole heart faint. From the
sole of the foot even unto the head there is no
soundness in it; but wounds, and bruises, and
putrefying sores: they have not been closed,
neither bound up, neither mollified with ointment.

Isaiah 1:4-6

The Lord says to His people, Israel, 'You're beaten
up and bruised and hurting and desolate and destroyed
because you have been laden, loaded with iniquity.' You
see, Pharaoh makes us labor, but sin makes us heavy-
laden. Sin weighs us down. David went through a season
of sin on more than one occasion. During one such time,
he wrote:

Oh there is no soundness in my flesh because of
thine anger; neither is there any rest in my bones
because of my sin. My iniquities are gone over my
head: as a heavy burden they are too heavy for
me. My wounds stink and are corrupt because of
my foolishness. I am troubled; I am bowed down
greatly; I go mourning all the day long. For my
loins are filled with a loathsome disease: and
there is no soundness in my flesh. I am feeble
and sore broken: I have roared by reason of the
disquietness of my heart.

Psalm 38:3-8

Sin will make you tired, gang. What does Jesus
say? He says, 'Whether you've been seduced and sucked
in by Pharaoh's mentality — working for the world and
finding it to be nothing but bricks and weariness — or
whether you've been heavy-laden with iniquity, come unto
Me.'

And I Will Give You Rest . . .

How?

A Word to the Weary

Take My Yoke upon You . . .

The word 'carpenter,' used in Matthew 13 to describe Joseph, is the word we use for a finish carpenter, rather than for a framer. Tradition has it that the carpenter shop where Jesus worked with His father, Joseph, specialized in making yokes. To yoke two oxen together, the skilled carpenter designed the yoke to fit each ox individually. Because there was always a lead ox yoked together with one that would follow, the yoke was designed in such a way that the lead ox would pull the greater weight. The follower, or assistant ox, was just to go with the flow. Thus, Jesus used an analogy well known to the people who listened to Him when He said not only, 'Come unto Me,' but, 'Yoke with Me. Let Me be the Lead Ox. Go with My flow. Don't try and figure out or change My direction. Let Me lead you.'

A story is told of a battleship cruising the Atlantic off the northern coast of Maine. One stormy evening, the Commander was notified, 'Sir, there's a light ahead. Oncoming vessel.'

'Signal the oncoming vessel: Change your courses ten degrees to the west,' ordered the Commander.

The message was sent. But a light flashed back, 'Change *your* course ten degrees to the east.'

'Signal again,' barked the Commander, 'change *your* course ten degrees to the west. I am an Admiral!'

The light flashed back, 'Change *your* course ten degrees to the east. I am a Seaman Third Class.'

By this time, the Admiral was incensed as he thundered, 'Signal again: Change *your* course ten degrees to the west. I am a battleship.'

And the message came back: 'Change *your* course ten degrees to the east. I am a lighthouse.'

So, too, as we impudently and impetuously say to the Lord, 'Lord, let's go my way,' He answers, 'No. We're going My way. I am the Lighthouse. I am the Light of the world, the Rock of your salvation, the Creator and Sustainer of your soul. I am the Alpha and the Omega, the One who knows the beginning from the end. Trust Me.'

And Learn of Me; for I Am Meek and Lowly in Heart . . .

This is the only autobiographical statement about His own personality that Jesus ever made. He didn't say, 'Learn of Me because I am majestic and mighty,' or 'Learn of Me because I am powerful and prominent.' He said, 'Learn of Me and what you will discover will refresh you. I am meek.'

What is meekness? Meekness is strength under control. Picture a big, gentle Saint Bernard surrounded by yapping, snapping, little Chihuahuas. Now, the Saint Bernard could open his mouth and chomp the Chihuahuas down in one gulp. He could knock them away with one swipe of his paw. But the powerful Saint Bernard patiently puts up with the yappers and snappers at his feet. That's meekness.

When I study the Scriptures and learn of Jesus, I am always amazed at His goodness, His grace, His kindness, His gentleness, and His meekness. 'Come to

Me,' He says 'you who have been burned out by Pharaoh, you who have been wearied by the folly of sin. Yoke with Me — don't try to maneuver Me, steer Me, or demand of Me. Learn of Me — for I am meek and lowly.' The result ?

And Ye Shall Find Rest in Your Soul . . .

You'll find what your heart is craving: Shabbat. Sabbath. Rest.

For My Yoke Is Easy, and My Burden Is Light

In Acts 15, questions arose concerning Gentile converts and whether or not they should follow the laws and the rituals and be circumcised. Peter gave this response:

> *Now therefore why tempt ye God, to put a yoke upon the neck of the disciples, which neither our fathers nor we were able to bear?*
>
> *Acts 15:10*

'My yoke is easy,' said Jesus.

It's not religion — it's relationship.

It's not Judaism — it's Jesus.

It's not the Law — it's love.

Sometimes I hear people say, 'I'm so burdened. It's so tough being a servant. It's so hard to be a brother, or a musician, or a witness.' Listen — if it's heavy, it's not His burden because His burden is light. If what I'm doing is tough and wearisome to me, then I know it's not the Lord who has placed that burden upon me. His burden is easy. His load is light.

Dear, weary saint, Jesus would say to you today, 'Come to Me. Don't labor under the burdens of Pharaoh.

You'll become weary if you do. Don't become heavy-laden under the bondage of sin. It will rob you of your energy. Don't become enslaved by the laws of the Pharisees. You'll be weighed down. Just come to Me. Yoke with Me. Learn of Me. And you'll find rest in your souls.'

Recognizing Our Redeemer

And in the fourth watch of the night Jesus went unto them, walking on the sea. And when the disciples saw him walking on the sea, they were troubled, saying, It is a spirit; and they cried out for fear. But straightway Jesus spake unto them, saying, Be of good cheer: it is I; be not afraid.

Matthew 14:25-27

IF THERE are animals in heaven, I am convinced my cat, Gabriel, will live in a mansion. Now, I'm not a big cat fan normally. In fact, I used to think all cats were somewhat demon-possessed. But I believe Gabriel is sanctified and saved! When he came to live with us, my daughter, Jessie, was about three years old, and she was determined that Gabriel the cat was Gabriel the horse. She rode him constantly. Then Christy came along. Christy was convinced Gabriel was a noisemaker. She pulled his tail day and night, and every time Gabriel screamed, she laughed. But Gabriel never retaliated. Now Mary's on the scene. Mary loves Gabriel and carries him around wherever she goes. Last week, however, we noticed he wasn't with her very much, so Tammy asked Mary, 'Where's Gabriel?'

'Oh, I'll get him!' Mary said as she ran to the other end of the house. She returned immediately, carrying Gabriel by his neck, like she always does.

'How did you know where he was?' asked Tammy.

'It was easy,' replied Mary. 'I've been keeping him in my drawer so I can find him when I want him.'

Sometimes that's the way we try to treat the Lord. We want to keep Him in our drawer so when we want Him or need Him, we'll know right where to find Him. The

Israelites tried the same thing. Fighting the Philistines in a brutal battle, as their losses mounted, so did their despair. Then someone had a brilliant idea: 'Let's bring in the Ark of the Covenant!' The Ark of the Covenant, a box about three feet long and two feet wide, was instrumental in tabernacle worship. 'Yeah, let's bring the Ark. The Ark will lead us in battle, and we'll be victorious!' When the Ark was brought into the Israelite camp, the Israelites cheered so loudly that their shout of triumph could be heard in the Philistine camp. But though the Israelites charged ahead with the Ark leading them, they were defeated resoundingly. And the Philistines captured the Ark (I Samuel 4).

The lesson? An obvious one. The people of God should not have tried to put God in a box saying, 'This box will represent God and we will have victory because of *it.*' Instead of looking to the Lord, they looked to the box, and were beaten badly.

If there is one thing many of us are learning, it is that the Lord works in mysterious ways. You just can't box Him in. He is predictably unpredictable. He comes at the unexpected time, in the unexpected way. Here in Matthew 14, the disciples are out in the storm, toiling at the oars, continuing obediently in the directive Jesus had given them to 'Go across the sea.' And while they are working and perspiring, Jesus is watching and praying — allowing them to go through the struggle, knowing the struggle would strengthen them. Finally, at 4 AM, knowing His disciples were feeling anxious and fearful, He comes to them walking on the water. He comes to them at the unexpected time in an unexpected way, and thinking He is a ghost, they freak out. So, too, I suggest to you that many times, Jesus comes to us as well, but, like the disciples, we don't recognize Him.

When your boyfriend or girlfriend calls and says, 'You know, I've been thinking. I really appreciate your personality. You've been a good friend, but . . .' Your heart stops and you say, 'This is frightening. It's a ghost.' When your boss calls you into the office and says, 'Don't bother to take off your coat,' you know what's coming and you think, 'It's a ghost! I'm scared.'

Oftentimes, when we, like the disciples, are obedient to the Lord, and toiling for the Lord, we call out, 'Lord, save me. I'm perishing. Lord, help me. I'm struggling.' Then He comes to us — but in ways that are totally surprising, refusing to be boxed in by our preconceptions of how and when He should appear. I would like us to look at four obstacles to seeing Jesus when He comes to us in the unexpected way, at the unexpected time.

Fear and Anxiety

Brothers and sisters, this is significant. The exhortation comes *before* the revelation. Scripture says in everything we are to give thanks, to rejoice evermore, for this is the will of God (Ephesians 5:20). If you begin to rejoice, to be of good cheer — suddenly you will see that it isn't a ghost, but it's Jesus drawing near. He's freeing you from that job, or from that relationship that will drag you down. It's the Lord coming to you in the storm.

When our hearts are full of fear and anxiety, what should we do? Look at Jesus' answer in the text before us. He said, 'Be of good cheer. It is I.' This intrigues me. He didn't say, 'It is I. Be of good cheer.' He said, 'Be of good cheer. It is I.' First, 'Be of good cheer' — an exhortation; then, 'It is I' — a revelation.

You who love the Lord and desire to do His will, next time fear and anxiety fill your heart, don't freak out — faith out. By faith, rejoice, and He will reveal Himself to you. He will walk on the water in the midst of your storm. Don't mistake Him for a ghost.

False Familiarity

Jesus came into His home town and there the people said of Him, 'Hey, isn't this the carpenter's son? And isn't Mary his mother? And don't we know His brothers and sisters?' They thought they knew Him, but their assumptions were mistaken. Matthew writes that Jesus could not do many mighty works there because of their unbelief (Matthew 13).

So, too, Jesus will come to you, gang, in people you know very well. Our tendency, however, is to say, 'That guy can't tell me anything. I know him.' 'I know her. She's my wife. She has nothing to say to me.' 'Him? He's only been a Christian six months. What could he possibly say to me?'

In reality, those people are Jesus coming to us. Jesus comes to us constantly, yet if we're not careful we'll say, 'I can't receive from her. I can't receive from him. I know them.' Paul said, 'I know no man after the flesh. I will no longer look at people with their faults and flaws and failures. I will see people only in Christ' (II Corinthians 5:16). When we begin to look at our husband, our wife, our friends, our kids, our brothers and sisters in the fellowship as people in Christ, realizing Jesus indwells them — suddenly we will lay hold of the most incredible understanding, profound revelation, and convicting challenges.

Why is it that we are so ready to receive from someone we esteem highly — a Billy Graham, or a Chuck Swindoll? Wouldn't it be radical if we saw *every* man in Christ? Jesus will come to you through the people closest to you, but if you're not careful, you'll miss Him.

Personal Tragedy

It was Easter morning. Mary Magdalene stood outside the sepulchre weeping, thinking the One speaking to her was a gardener (John 20:15). Sometimes the person who comes to us in time of tragedy, the person who ministers to us most effectively is not an angel or an apostle. In times of tragedy, Jesus will come to you in the most ordinary of people — the gardeners. Mary, no doubt, thought, 'If anyone is going to give me understanding, it will be Peter, John, or the angels at the tomb. They will help me.' But Jesus came to Mary directly and she mistook Him for a gardener.

Maybe you're going through a time of real personal tragedy. In those times of weeping and crying, be careful because sometimes you'll miss Jesus coming to you very personally. You will think He should come as Peter or as John or as an angel sent from heaven. But you know how He'll come? Through a very common person you wouldn't have expected. And if your antenna isn't up, you'll miss Him. You'll mistake Him as being insignificant and unimportant.

After going through a time of tragedy in my own life, I have a new appreciation for the gardeners — for people who don't have apostolic stature, or angelic revelation — common people who did the most precious things and said the most comforting words. Too often we think we need to see the pastor, a staff member, an elder, or an angel when we should really be looking for the gardener. Look for the person you thought wouldn't have much to say or much to offer. That's where the deep, beautiful ministry of Jesus will often flow most freely.

Despair and Despondency

In Luke 24, we read the account of two followers of Jesus walking on the Road to Emmaus, who were depressed and despondent following the death of their Master. As Jesus joined them and asked the reason for their sorrow, they said, 'Are you a stranger here? Don't you know what's happening? Where have you been?' Then Jesus began to rebuke them gently and lovingly for their lack of faith. Beginning with Moses and going through the prophets, He told them how all of the Scriptures foretold His death and resurrection. When you are depressed and despondent, the Lord will come to you. Initially, however, you might feel He's a stranger . . .

Going through a time of emotional turmoil and great difficulty, unable to sleep, I turned on the television to a Christian station and watched a preacher, whom I had previously thought was very strange. He wasn't into heresy doctrinally, but his whole approach to the ministry was kind of weird. Normally, I wouldn't have given him the time of day, but this particular night, being the only thing on at 3 AM, I listened to him. And guess what? His words spoke precisely and powerfully to my exact situation.

The Lord will often come through the person you might have previously thought strange. The eyes of the travelers on the Emmaus Road were opened when Jesus broke bread with them. So, too, when we break bread in Communion, we realize we are one Body, all partaking of the same Lord, all cleansed by His blood. Our differences become irrelevant when we break bread because suddenly our eyes are opened and we see Jesus.

Francis of Assisi had a burning desire to see with his eyes the One whose voice he heard in his heart. One day as he was riding his horse, he saw some lepers at a distance and felt a prompting within him to get off his horse and go kiss one of them. Now, leprosy was a hideous disease, and one which Francis particularly loathed and feared. Yet obediently, he got off his horse, went to the most grotesque of the lepers, and hugged and kissed him. At that moment, something incredible happened: The face of the leper was transformed into the face of Jesus Christ. Francis learned that day that Jesus appears in an unexpected way, through an unexpected person.

Fear and anxiety, false familiarity, personal tragedy, despair and despondency will keep you from recognizing your Redeemer. But if you say, 'I will watch for You, Lord, in the storm. I will praise Your Name and embrace this difficulty, trusting You are revealing Yourself to me; I will receive from those whom I think I know so well. I will take their words as Yours. I will listen for Your voice in the common person, in the gardener, rather than waiting for an apostle or an angel to speak my name; I will embrace the stranger, who walks alongside me, and as we break bread at Your table, I will see Your face' — you will see Jesus come to you in ways and through people you never expected.

Sender of the Storm

When Jesus therefore perceived that they would come and take him by force, to make him a king, he departed again into a mountain himself alone. And when even was now come, his disciples went down unto the sea, And entered into a ship, and went over the sea toward Capernaum. And it was now dark, and Jesus was not come to them. And the sea arose by reason of a great wind that blew. So when they had rowed about five and twenty or thirty furlongs, they see Jesus walking on the sea, and drawing nigh unto the ship: and they were afraid. But he saith unto them, It is I: be not afraid. Then they willingly received him into the ship: and immediately the ship was at the land whither they went.

John 6:15-21

DENNIS AVERY, Music Minister at St. Paul's Church of Christ, walked into the 3rd–4th grade Sunday School class just in time to hear the president of the class pray. 'Dear God,' said the nine-year-old, 'bless our mothers and our fathers, and our sisters and brothers. And bless the teachers. And, oh, by the way, God, take care of Yourself because if anything happens to You, we're all sunk.'

The text before us makes it clear that Jesus is unsinkable. Truly, our Lord and Friend is our Savior in the storm, who will come when the hour is darkest, when the danger is greatest. But I want you to see something else here this morning: Jesus Christ is not only the Savior in the storm, but He is also the Sender of the storm; for in Matthew's account of this same story, Jesus commanded the disciples to cross the Sea of Galilee — knowing all the while a storm would be coming (Matthew 14:22).

Why would Jesus be the Sender of the very storm you're going through presently? Why would He allow the wind to rise, and the waves to beat on your little boat? I submit four reasons why Jesus Christ, our Captain, our Savior in the storm, is also the Sender of the storm.

He Sends Storms to Give Us New Direction

They that go down to the sea in ships, that do business in great waters; these see the works of the Lord, and his wonders in the deep. For he commandeth, and raiseth the stormy wind, which lifteth up the waves thereof, they mount up to the heaven, they go down again to the depths: their soul is melted because of trouble. They reel to and fro, and stagger like a drunken man, and are at their wits' end. Then they cry unto the Lord in their trouble, and he bringeth them out of their distresses.

Psalm 107:23-28

The Lord creates storms to cause sailors to come to their wits' end. You see, in times of pride and pomposity, we think, 'I'm captain of my ship, master of my fate' — until a storm suddenly and savagely comes into our life. Then we find ourselves finally calling out to the One for whom we had no time previously, or didn't think we had need of personally. Paul says it's the goodness of God which leads men to repentance (Romans 2:4). That's the ideal, but that's not always how it works practically. With those who don't respond to His goodness, God must deal radically in order to get their attention.

In Kilgore, Texas, a year ago, a man was rescued from the scene of an automobile accident. After his car crashed into a telephone pole, some passersby lifted the unconscious man out of his car and took him to a gas station half a block away, where they called an ambulance. Before the ambulance arrived, however, the man came to, looked around, and tried to stand. Although those who had rescued him held him down, with incredible strength he tried to get out of their grasp until he lost consciousness once more. Only later did it become clear why the man struggled so. You see, the gas station to which he was taken was a Shell station, and when he initially regained consciousness, his rescuers happened to be standing around him in such a way that they blocked the letter S on the Shell sign from his view. Thus, he woke up, thinking he was in hell.

'What does it profit a man,' Jesus asked, 'if he gain the whole world, but lose his soul?' (Mark 8:36). Sometimes the Lord may have to put us in a crash, a difficulty, a shocking situation to get our attention because He's more concerned about our eternal state than He is about our present comfort. Truly, He sends storms to bring us to our wits' end — that we might call upon Him, and change direction.

He Sends Storms to Give Us Necessary Correction

> . . . I cried by reason of mine affliction unto the Lord, and he heard me; out of the belly of hell cried I, and thou heardest my voice. For thou hadst cast me into the deep, in the midst of the seas; and the floods compassed me about: all thy billows and thy waves passed over me.
>
> *Jonah 2:2-3*

God wanted to use Jonah greatly in Nineveh. But Jonah found a ship going in the opposite direction. Interesting how that works. Whenever you want to backslide, whenever you want to turn away, whenever you want to sail in the opposite direction, guess who is in port with a ship all ready to go? Satan. Satan never says, 'You want to backslide? Great! Where's a ship? Somebody, get me a ship!' Nope. He's already got the ships in port, engines revved, sails set. Right now, if you want to jump on it, Satan has a ship waiting for you. But the problem is, like Jonah, you'll pay for it.

Telling me about his diet, a man said, 'It seemed like the Lord spoke to my heart about cutting down. But one day, I thought it might be His will that I have a donut; so I asked Him if it were really His will to give me a parking place right in front of the donut shop. And sure enough, after only the third time around the block, there it was!'

Maybe some of you are circling around the block right now saying, 'Well, Lord, if You want me to get involved with him . . .' or, 'If you want me to go there. . .' It'll probably happen, because Satan always has a ship ready. But know this: If you're running from God, or trying to rationalize what you know is not His best for you, a storm is sure to follow.

He Sends Storms to Give Us Needed Protection

And they that had eaten were about five thousand men, beside women and children. And straightway Jesus constrained his disciples to get into a ship, and to go before him unto the other side, while he sent the multitudes away.

Matthew 14:21-22

The people had been fed miraculously, and now they wanted Jesus to rule them politically. Knowing this would sound like the moment His disciples had been waiting for, realizing it would seem like the fulfillment of their dreams, Jesus sent them away for their own protection.

The Fairfax County, Virginia, Fire Department received a shipment of high-tech helmets. Brightly-colored, scuff-resistant, adjustable-strapped, they were incredible works of art, complete with $500 price tags. There was only one problem: they melted when they got near heat.

Likewise, the Lord has to say to you and me, 'What are you doing? You're building your little kingdom. You're getting your house together, and your car all shiny; you're involved with this gadget and that gizmo, with this hobby and the other activity — but they're not going to take the heat.' When our lives are tested with fire at the judgment seat of Christ that which is wood, hay, or stubble will burn. Only that which is gold, silver, or precious stone will remain (I Corinthians 3:12-15). So what does the Lord do? He says, 'Jon, to get your mind off the material world, I'm sending you into a storm where you will wrestle with issues and struggle with difficulties. I'm watching over you, praying for you, and living right inside of you — but it's a struggle that you're going to have to go through in order to shift your focus from the temporal to the eternal.'

He Sends Storms to Nurture Perfection

And as they spake unto the people, the priests, and the captain of the temple, and the Sadducees, came upon them, being grieved that they taught the people, and preached through Jesus the resurrection from the dead. And they laid hands on them, and put them in hold unto the next day: for it was now eventide. Howbeit many of them which heard the word believed; and the number of the men was about five thousand.

Acts 4:1-4

After feeding five thousand people, Jesus sent His disciples into a storm while He ascended to a mountain

(Matthew 14:23). I believe He did this to prepare them for the time that He would ascend not to a mountain, but all the way to heaven. In Acts 4, we see the five thousand mentioned once more — not being fed, but being saved. And immediately after the five thousand were saved, a storm of persecution broke out that was so brutal the disciples were cast into prison. Thus, the storm they went through for a couple of hours on the Sea of Galilee, described in the book of John, was simply preparatory for what would happen in the storm of persecution, which would follow in Acts.

Our Captain sees what tomorrow holds. That's why He says, 'As difficult as this might seem, it's absolutely necessary to prepare you and perfect you for what is coming.' Suffice to say, there were storms I previously went through which were absolutely necessary for the storms that would follow a decade later. Gang, the storms you and I are presently going through are necessary to enable us to navigate what lies ahead.

So what should we do? Should we freak out? Give up? Turn back? Should we take a ship in the opposite direction? No. We should follow the example of the disciples, embrace the storm, and stay the course, knowing Jesus will appear to us at exactly the right moment, saying, 'It is I; be not afraid.'

Fellow sailors, be of good cheer, and rejoice that the Sender of the storm is also our Savior *in* the storm — for without Him, we'd all be sunk!

But God

But God, who is rich in mercy, for his great love wherewith he loved us . . .

Ephesians 2:4

ASKED WHAT I enjoy most about the ministry, I was surprised by my own answer. 'What I enjoy most about the ministry are the messes,' I said, 'just watching the wonderful things the Lord creates from the muddle and mayhem, in which we continually find ourselves.'

It's been this way from the very beginning. You see, Genesis 1:1 records that in the beginning God created the heavens and the earth. But there's a troubling phrase in verse 2: 'And the earth was without form and void.' Why is this troubling? Because Isaiah 45:18 says God created the earth *not* in vain, but to be inhabited. So what happened? It would seem as though God created a perfect earth, and then the earth went through such a cataclysmic change between Genesis 1:1 and Genesis 1:2 that it became 'without form and void.' What was the cause of this change? Many Bible scholars believe it was the result of Satan's entry on this planet after he and one-third of the angels were cast out of heaven. Thus, the creation of Genesis 1:1 was possibly so altered by Satan's rebellion that it caused the earth to tilt on its axis and usher in the Ice Age. So it is that even from the very beginning of time, we see a dismal, dark mess. But Scripture goes on to say that when God said, 'let there be light,' what was once 'without form and void' began to become something incredibly wonderful — the amazing earth upon which we live.

Not only does God re-create the world around us, but also the world in which we live. You see, according to Ephesians 2:1, we were all 'without form and void,' dead. But according to verse 4, just as He did at creation, God moved in and revived us. Perhaps you feel that the axis of your world has tilted, or that you're living in the cold blast of a perpetual Ice Age, or that darkness surrounds and abounds. 'Yes, you're a mess,' Paul would say to you. Then he would add the two words, which made all the difference at the creation of the physical world, and will make all the difference in your world as well: *But God.*

Abraham and his wife Sarah were once again traveling, and Abraham once again was fearful. Why? Because Sarah was so beautiful he knew Abimelech, the king of the region through which they passed, would want to kill him in order to add Sarah to his harem. 'Tell him you're my sister,' Abraham said. 'He'll take you away — but at least I won't die.' Sure enough, 'Abimelech, king of Gerar, sent and took Sarah' (Genesis 20:2). '*But God* came to Abimelech in a dream by night, and said to him, Behold Thou art a dead man, for the woman whom thou has taken; for she is a man's wife' (Genesis 20:3). Abraham messed it up royally; his marriage teetered on disaster, literally. *But God* moved in unexpectedly, unpredictably, miraculously, and rescued them both.

People say to me, 'My wife just doesn't understand.' 'My husband is an idiot.' 'My marriage is a mess.' 'What do I do?' I listen to their stories, shrug my shoulders, and say, 'Beats me. I don't have a clue. *But God* — somehow God is going to come through for you. I don't know how. I don't know when. But I know *Him*. God is gonna break through somehow.'

'Your dad ripped me off,' Jacob said to his wives, Leah and Rachel, after being shortchanged by Laban one too many times. '*But God* suffered him not to hurt me' (Genesis 31:7). 'No wonder in-law problems rank third in the struggles of married couples,' says the weary couple. 'We can't seem to please either of ours. What should we do?' 'I have no idea,' I say, '*But God* used Jacob's ordeal with Laban to eventually change Jacob from 'the heel snatcher' to Israel 'the one governed by God.'

On his sickbed, Jacob was no doubt reminded of his own deceit repeated in the lives of his sons gathered around him. Perhaps realizing that his time to impact them positively was growing short, it was with an air of resignation that he said, 'Behold I die.' Yet as he uttered the last word of that sentiment, hope reclaimed his heart as he added . . . *but God* shall be with you and bring you to the land of your fathers' (Genesis 48:21). 'What can I do about my son? It's as if I don't even exist in his life. Yes, I made mistakes raising him, but what can I do now?' 'I don't know,' I say. '*But God* will be with him just as He was with Jacob's sons, to bring him to the land of his fathers, to somehow, some way, bring him back home.'

After being thrown in a pit by his own brothers, he was sold into slavery. Joseph was forsaken by his family and without hope completely. *But God* moved in miraculously and elevated him to the position of Prime Minister in one of the greatest empires in history (Genesis 50:20). Everyone's against me — even my own family,' cries the broken-hearted young man. 'What do I do?' I listen to his story, and say, 'I don't know. *But God* . . . God was with Joseph and God will be with you.'

Initially, they could have taken a much more direct route to the Promised Land, '*but God* led the people about through the way of the wilderness of the Red Sea in order that they wouldn't have to deal with the Philistines (Exodus 14:17-18). People ask questions about finding God's will more than they do about anything else. 'What should I do?' they wonder. 'I could give you the logical, practical answer,' I tell them. '*But God* alone knows the true answer. And He will creatively, clearly, lovingly lead you — just as He did the Israelites.'

After killing 1,000 Philistines with the jawbone of an ass, Samson was so thirsty he thought he would die. '*But God* clave an hollow place that was in the jaw, and there came water out of it; and when he and drunk, his spirit came again, and he revived . . .' (Judges 15:19). 'I'm so dry spiritually,' she says. 'I come to church and I'm dry. I pray and I'm dry. I study the Word and I'm dry. What am I doing wrong?' 'Beats me,' I say. '*But God* hears your prayer and will revive you perhaps in a way you least expect it.'

Although Saul was king of Israel, he knew it was actually David who had the anointing of God. Realizing that killing him was Saul's solution to the problem, David hid in the wilderness where 'Saul sought him every day. *But God* delivered him not into his hand' (1 Samuel 23:14). What temptations, what sin, what Saul is trying to track you down and do you in? You'll never be able to elude it on your own, *but God* can establish, strengthen, settle you (I Peter 5:10), and give you victory. 'Oh, but you don't know the Saul that's chasing me,' you say. 'It's a very real temptation, an incredibly powerful problem.' 'Perhaps,' I say. '*But God* will not allow you to be tempted beyond what you're able, and will provide a way of escape every single time you're tempted' (I Corinthians 10:13).

Precious brother, dear sister, God who is rich in mercy and full of love, will break through your situation if you'll allow him. The mess you're in may be real, the struggle may be exhausting, the trial overwhelming — but the message is yet more powerful:

But God . . .

But God . . .

But *God* . . .

Shake It Off!

And when Paul had gathered a bundle of sticks, and laid them on the fire, there came a viper out of the heat, and fastened on his hand. And when the barbarians saw the venomous beast hang on his hand, they said among themselves, No doubt this man is a murderer, whom, though he hath escaped the sea, yet vengeance suffereth not to live. And he shook off the beast into the fire, and felt no harm.

Acts 28:3-5

HE WAS not speaking theologically or theoretically, for Paul was in a pretty tough spot personally. Sailing across the Mediterranean Sea to Rome, a storm began to beat and batter the boat full of prisoners, of which he was one. Finally, after many days, the 270 soldiers, sailors, and prisoners aboard were all cast into the sea. Some grabbed on to the splintered remains of the ship, some started swimming; but miraculously all made it to the shore of Mileta, present-day Malta. The 'barbarians' on the beach, showing these waterlogged newcomers 'no little kindness' (Acts 28:2), lit fires to warm them. And Paul, ever looking for an opportunity to serve others, joined in as he gathered sticks to fuel the flames. But lurking in one of the bundles was a deadly viper, which leapt out and bit him. When Paul merely shook off the snake into the fire, the local Miletans, who had initially thought Paul was cursed to suffer such a fate, now thought him a god.

Paul used the opportunity to share the True and Living God with the audience, who was eager to hear from this one who had been bitten by the same type of snake, which doubtless had claimed the lives of many of their family members and friends. 'Make my life count,' we plead. 'OK,' says the Lord as He allows us to be smitten by the snake of sickness and sorrow. 'I will allow this to happen because the locals — the natives in the Rogue

Valley — are watching to see if there are any answers, any solutions, any hope for them.'

A.W. Tozer, spiritual giant of the previous generation, was right when he said, 'Before God can use a person greatly, He must allow that person to be hurt deeply.' Why? Is it because God is cruel? Does He enjoy seeing us in pain? No. The issue is not cruelty. The issue is ministry because there are two essential, non-negotiable prerequisites for those who desire to be used by God . . .

Compassion for People

We may have our theology down pat, but if our hearts are not full of compassion for people, what we say will not be fully received because the old adage is true: People don't care how much we know until they know how much we care. How can I have compassion? By absorbing the bite of the same snake which bites others. There is no other way.

Therefore, God puts us in situations and tribulations, hard places and tough times, in order that we might develop compassion for people who are also experiencing difficulties — in order that we might be able to say, 'I *know* what you're going through.'

There are those who have compassion for people, who can put an arm around them and cry with them. And although that is good and necessary, it is not enough . . .

Confidence in God

Many Christians have compassion for people, but it is at the expense of God's reputation. 'I really feel for you,' they say. 'I don't know why this is happening' — the implication being, 'Where is God?' On the other hand, one who truly ministers will say, 'God is *good*. Here's what He did in my life, and here's what He will do for you. Put your confidence in Him.'

Quite frankly, gang, I think we should be more concerned about the reputation of our perfect Heavenly Father than about our own relatability. He has promised never let us be tempted above that which we are able, and that all things are working together for good. He has promised He will never leave us, and He has told us to rejoice in Him always. Such is the example of Paul. Because he had endured beatings in prison, storms at sea, and snakebites on the beach, he had compassion for the problems of others; and because he had experienced God's faithfulness through it all, he never compromised his belief that God is good.

'Well,' you might be thinking, 'if the only way to have compassion for people and confidence in God is to be bitten by a snake or two, then count me out. I'll be an every-other-Sunday believer, but don't ask me to get involved in ministry or service.' You can choose to be left out if you wish — but you must understand this: You will still be bitten by the same snake.

Why? It all has to do with the snake in the Garden of Eden. That is why there is starvation and sickness in Somalia. That is why there is war in Bosnia. That is why there are earthquakes in China. And that is why there is pain in your world. 'What is God doing?' people cry when, in fact, it is not God's doing at all.

Having just encouraged His followers to develop faith, when the evening was come, Jesus said to His disciples, 'Let us go over to the other side' (Mark 4:35).

But when a storm arose on the Sea of Galilee, the terrified disciples woke Jesus, who was asleep in the boat. 'Peace, be still,' or literally, 'be muzzled,' He said — the same term He employed when speaking to demons.

Thus, the insurance companies have it all wrong. The flood or earthquake which threatens your house is no more an 'act of God' than the storm which bullied the disciples. They're acts of Satan, who was given permission by mankind to wreak havoc upon the earth when Adam rebelled in the Garden. You see, the disciples weren't the only ones on the Sea of Galilee when the storm arose; they were just the ones who had Jesus on board. Consequently, whether you decide to engage in ministry or not, you will still experience the snakebite of sickness, or the storm of sorrow because the whole world has been polluted by the fallout of Adam's bomb. In this life, everyone experiences equal difficulty because everyone has been bitten (1 Corinthians 10:13).

After murmuring yet again, the children of Israel were dying by the thousands from the fiery serpents God sent to bite them. 'What do we do now?' cried Moses. 'Make a brass snake on a brass pole,' God answered, 'and put it in the middle of the camp so that anyone who is bitten can look at the serpent hanging there and be made whole.' Many were healed. Others, however, thinking it useless, perished in their stupidity (Numbers 21). Centuries passed, and all the while, no doubt, people were wondering what was the deal with the brass serpent. Then came a Rabbi from Galilee who explained it all when He said, 'As Moses lifted up the serpent in the wilderness, so must the Son of Man be lifted up' (John 3:14-15).

So, too, it might take a year or two, or five or ten — or maybe an eternity — until we understand why we were bitten by the snake of sorrow, smitten with the sting of despair. But when we see Him who was made sin for us, it will all make sense. As in Numbers 14, some will refuse to look upon Him, saying instead, 'Look at my snake. Can you believe how bad this is?' Help me, help me.' But others will follow the example of Paul and will shake the snake of Satan's sting into the fire of God's promise.

Our flight landed in Orlando at 11:30 PM. There was supposed to be a rental car ready for Peter John and me at the airport; but evidently our reservation had been mixed up, so we found ourselves on a bus headed to the 'vacation center' where surplus cars were stored. Upon arriving there, it was obvious that 'vacation center' was just another name for 'one-step-above-junkyard.' It being midnight by now, and without having any other recourse, we walked into the office to pick up our car. Behind the counter was a tired-looking man. Perhaps expecting us to complain, his countenance changed as I began joking with him and he with me — especially when he learned that I was in the ministry. 'I haven't met any Christians like you,' said this Brooklyn Jew named Barry.

Half an hour later, nearing 1 AM, he said, 'I think I've got a car for you. It's a brand-new, fully-loaded, convertible Mustang with no miles on it. You guys want it?' The next day found Peter John and me cruising the 900 miles to Pensacola with the top down, hearing people say, 'Nice car,' all day long.

It was just a once-in-a-lifetime experience. If I had walked into the vacation center saying, 'What's the deal?

Where's my car? You guys really blew it,' would we have had that experience? I wonder.

Turn your miseries into Mustangs, saint. Sure, things go wrong, but whether they be little inconveniences or major heartbreaks, trust in the Lord. Realize they are opportunities to learn compassion for people and to gain confidence in God. Whether it be a big python or a little garden variety, shake off the snake and see God use you in the lives of the amazed barbarians and rental-car guys who watch you.

It's All for Good

And we know that all things work together for good to them that love God, to them who are the called according to his purpose.

Romans 8:28

CERTAIN THINGS we *don't* know — like how honeybees fly when, theoretically, their wings are too short and too light to support them when carrying pollen. Some things we *can't* know — like the day or hour of the Rapture (Matthew 25:13). Or, who will be in heaven (Matthew 13:24-30). Several things we *should* know — like the fact that Jesus is coming again (I Thessalonians 4:13), and the manifestation of spiritual gifts (I Corinthians 12). But there is one thing we *do* know . . .

The Promise Given *to* Us

'And we know that all things work together for good to them that love God, to them who are called according to his purpose,' wrote Paul (Romans 8:28).

How do we know this?

Because it's in the Bible.

Alright. But what about the guys in Rome to whom Paul was writing? They had never heard of Romans 8:28. How, then, could Paul assume they knew its truth?

The Price Paid *for* Us

A few verses down, in Romans 8:32, Paul wrote, 'God spared not His own Son but delivered Him up for you and me.' If He loved you enough to send His Son to be slaughtered in your stead, don't you know God will do what's good for you continually? When I begin to doubt the love of God, or wonder if things are really working out for good, all I need to do is look to Calvary and see Jesus dying for me.

The Peace *within* Us

God's goodness was known and understood by Old Testament saints long before the Cross of Calvary. How? Because, deep within their hearts, in the midst of tragedy, in the face of difficulty, all those who love God know that all things are truly working together for good — even though at first they question God's goodness.

There is a man in the Old Testament who did this very thing. Turn to Genesis 42, and see how he initially deceived himself by thinking God was not working everything together for good in his own life.

Here's the situation: Jacob had twelve sons. Although he loved them all, one was especially dear to him. His name? Joseph. Jealous of his standing with his father, Joseph's brothers threw him into a pit, where they were going to leave him to die until one of the brothers suggested they could make some money off him if they sold him as a slave. So sell him they did, after which they smeared blood all over his coat, and took it to Jacob, saying, 'Bad news, Dad. Joseph was eaten by wild animals.'

Meanwhile, through an incredible series of events, Joseph became Prime Minister of Egypt — number two to Pharaoh himself. When famine hit Israel, Jacob called his sons together and said, 'I've heard there's a man in Egypt who has food. Go ask him if we can buy some grain.' So his sons, ten in number, appeared before the Prime Minister, whom they didn't recognize as their brother.

'Why are you here?' asked Joseph.

'We're here to buy grain, your Highness.'

'I think you're lying,' said Joseph. 'I think you've come to spy out the land.'

'No,' insisted his brothers. 'We're brothers. In fact, there were twelve of us originally, but one is dead, and the youngest is at home.'

'If that's true,' countered Joseph, 'Go bring your youngest brother to me. That will validate your story. Meanwhile, the oldest of you will stay in prison as security until the youngest one is brought back.'

What was Jacob's answer to this demand? 'Joseph is not, and Simeon is not, and ye will take Benjamin away; all these things are against me' (Genesis 42:36).

What does Romans 8 say? 'All things work for good.' What does Jacob declare? 'Everything is working against me. Simeon, is a hostage. Joseph is dead. And my son Benjamin is soon to disappear.' Interesting. Jacob was completely wrong: Joseph was in perfect health. Benjamin would return. Simeon would be released.

Yet even though Jacob said, 'Everything is against me,' I suggest to you that deep down inside, he didn't believe it. Why? Because in the next chapter we read that the brothers did indeed return to Egypt — with Benjamin in tow. Knowing Jacob, if he *really* believed Benjamin would die in Egypt, he would not have allowed Benjamin to go. Clever, cunning Jacob would have figured out another way. But his sending Benjamin proves he didn't *really* believe everything was working against him.

Joseph identified himself to his brothers, and as they fell at his feet, he said, 'Don't fear. Although you meant evil against me, God meant it for good' (Genesis 50:20). Here's the question: How am I going to react to difficulty? Am I going to be like Jacob and say, 'All things are working against me' — even though I know in my heart such is not the case? Or, am I going to be like Joseph and say, 'Man may have meant this for evil, but God meant it for good'?

Unfortunately, all too often, I choose the sniveling of Jacob over the security of Joseph. Why? To elicit sympathy. What is it about our flesh that wants people to think we have it tough? What is in us that wants people to think we have it hard? While this may seem an insignificant quirk, in reality it borders on blasphemy because in getting you to feel sorry for me, I get you to question God's goodness, provision, and protection in my life. Thus, your pity for me is at God's expense.

Who am I going to be? I can be self-indulgent and allow God to be cast in a bad light even though I know in my heart the promise given to me, the price paid for me, the peace available within me. I can deny all of that and say, 'I want you to feel sorry for me. Listen to my tragedy.' Or I can say, 'I will not dishonor this good, gracious, loving God, who has been so kind to me, so good for me. He's my Creator and my Father. Therefore, I will not bring shame to His Name in seeking sympathy from anyone.' That is called the fear of the Lord. It's saying, 'Father, I care more about Your reputation than I do about getting sympathy from the congregation. I don't want them to think questioningly, negatively, or blasphemously of You.'

Where are the men and women in the Rogue Valley who say, 'We fear God. We will not snivel. God is good and we know deep within our hearts that He is working all things together for good'?

Here's the question: In the name of compassion, are you one who constantly weeps with others? Perhaps what we need in the Christian community during this time of self-centered Christianity are men and women who say, 'I fear God. So, Dear brother, precious sister, even if you don't understand — even if you think this is cold-hearted or lacking compassion — you *know* that this difficulty or tragedy will work for good. Stand on that knowledge. Cling to it. I will weep for you if you don't get it. But I'm not going to weep with you as you question God. He's too good for that.'

May God give us wisdom.

May God give us peace.

May God give us understanding.

All things work together for good to them that love God, to them called according to His purpose.

I know it.

So do you.

In the Pits

And Benaiah the son of Jehoiada, the son of a valiant man, of Kabzeel, who had done many acts, he slew two lionlike men of Moab: he went down also and slew a lion in the midst of a pit in time of snow: And he slew an Egyptian, a goodly man: and the Egyptian had a spear in his hand; but he went down to him with a staff, and plucked the spear out of the Egyptian's hand, and slew him with his own spear.

II Samuel 23:20-21

THE TITLE alone propelled Erma Bombeck's *If Life Is A Bowl Of Cherries, What Am I Doing In The Pits?* to the top of the best-seller list because it's a question to which we can all relate. Truly, each one of us from time to time finds ourselves in the proverbial pits. The Psalmist declared that at one point, he was dwelling *continually* in a horrible pit. But he was rescued. He was delivered. And his feet were set upon a solid rock (Psalm 40). So, too, there was a time when each of us was dwelling in a horrible pit — that of not knowing why we existed or where we were headed. But the Lord graciously reached down to us, rescued us, and placed us upon a Rock, Jesus Christ. And yet, even though we have been rescued out of the horrible pit, we find ourselves from time to time in lesser pits . . .

When I was about 16 years old, my older brother, Dave, and I got new 10-speed Gitane bicycles. Mine was white, Dave's blue. With our younger brother, Jimmy, on his brown Schwinn Varsity, we set off from our home in San Jose over the mountains to the beach at Santa Cruz. The grade being brutally steep, when we reached the summit, we were exhausted. Nonetheless, Dave proposed a race down to the beach, so off we went. Being the best cyclist, Dave led the way. I followed, with Jimmy bringing up the rear. 'There's no way I'm going to win,' I thought,

'Dave's got that sewn up. But as long as I can beat Jimmy...'

Just then, my peripheral vision caught sight of an ominous brown Schwinn Varsity on my tail. So I decided to release the brakes all the way and just go for it. Sailing down the hill towards the bottom of the incline, I thought I was home free when suddenly I found myself launched like a rocket through the air. Landing in a mud bank, I sat by the side of the road dazed and covered in mud.

About ten minutes later, realizing I was nowhere in sight, Dave and Jimmy came back up the hill.

'What happened?' they said.

'I don't know,' I answered.

So we surveyed the road for a clue, and discovered a peach pit in the middle of the road, which I had hit in such a way that it caused my wheel to collapse. It was something small, something seemingly insignificant. But in reality, it was sufficient to knock me off my course.

So, too, sometimes as we're cruising down the road in our Christian walk, there can be something that seems small, insignificant, which throws us off course and causes us to be in the proverbial pits. What are we to do at such a time? The same things Benaiah did . . .

Schooled For the Pit

And Benaiah the son of Jehoiada, the son of a valiant man, of Kabzeel, who had done many acts . . .

II Samuel 23:20

Scripture tells us Benaiah was the son of a 'valiant man,' a strong man, a hero. Truly, the most important ministry we'll ever have is with our own kids . . .

One snowy day, a man wrestling with alcoholism, finding his liquor cabinet empty, walked out his front door to refill his supply. As he walked down the sidewalk, he sensed someone following him, so he turned around. And sure enough, putting his little feet in the footprints of his father was his four-year-old boy.

'What are you doing?' asked the man.

'I'm walking in your footsteps!' replied his son.

So convicted was this father by his son's statement that he vowed never again to touch alcohol.

We have little guys walking in our footsteps, doing what we do more than doing what we say. Benaiah's dad must have realized this as he walked valiantly before his son.

Struggle in the Pit

He slew two lion-like men of Moab; he went down also and slew a lion in the midst of a pit in time of snow:

II Samuel 23:20

The Moabites were a group of people who continually hassled and irritated the people of God. Thus, Benaiah was brought face to face with irritations, hassles, plagues and problems as part of the preparation for what was to come next. You see, after Benaiah struggled with the lion-like men of Moab, he slew a lion in the midst of a pit.

Maybe you're wondering why the Lord has allowed little irritations to pick at you: little hassles, little plagues, little problems to annoy you. God being the Alpha and Omega, He knows the beginning from the end and sees what's down the road. Consequently, these lion-like men were simply preparatory to strengthen Benaiah for the lion.

Husband, if your wife is constantly picking at you, embrace her. She's part of God's preparation process. Wife, if your husband is really irritating, embrace him. He's part of God's preparation promise for you. Kids, if your parents are hard to understand, embrace them. They're part of God's preparation program for you.

Victory in the Pit

And he slew an Egyptian, a goodly man: and the Egyptian had a spear in his hand; but he went down to him with a staff, and plucked the spear out of the Egyptian's hand, and slew him with his own spear.

II Samuel 23:20-21

What was Benaiah's secret? Throughout Scripture, the Egyptian is symbolic of the flesh, which seeks to dominate us and is energized by Satan. In II Samuel 23, Benaiah took the Egyptian's own spear, and thrust it right through the 'goodly', or big, Egyptian. I like this because in it there is a very wonderful, powerful, practical principle about how you and I can get victory in the pits. That is, we must take the offensive. We must grab the very weapon with which the Egyptian would seek to pin us to the wall, the very spear with which he would seek to destroy us, and thrust it back at him.

What spears does Satan hurl at us when we're in the pit? I'll name two . . .

The first is that of condemnation: 'You're not praying enough. You're not going to church enough. You're not reading the Bible enough, giving enough, devoted enough, teaching Sunday school enough. You're watching TV too much, reading the newspaper too much, relaxing too much.' Because he accuses us day and night (Revelation 12:10), if you're not careful, you'll find yourself in the pit, slain by his accusations.

What are we to do? Revelation 12 goes on to say that they overcame Satan by the blood of the Lamb and the word of their testimony. Therefore, when this lion roars at me, seeking to keep me in the pit because of condemnation, I am learning to say, 'You're right, Satan, but only half right because I'm even worse than you think. But while you are accusing me, Jesus is excusing me. While you are nailing me, He was nailed for me. While you are pointing the finger at me, He is pouring His blood out upon me.' And as I bathe in God's grace and enjoy His goodness, you know what happens? The weapon of accusation and condemnation is turned against Satan and he flees (James 4:7).

The second spear with which the enemy will seek to nail us is that of criticism. When criticism is hurled my way, I am slowly learning to say, 'Lord, what can I learn from it?' You see, every time you're criticized, you can either become defensive about it or enlarged by it. May the Lord help us to be those who say, 'I'm going to embrace this criticism because in it there is some element of truth, which the Lord is drawing to my attention. Somehow I have miscommunicated, demonstrated a negative attitude, or erred in some way to bring about this criticism; so Lord, help me to learn what it is in order that I can grow through it.' When you do this, suddenly the giant spear of criticism is turned back on the enemy, and down he goes.

Gang, when you find yourself in the pit, either doing battle against the small irritations of the lion-like men of Moab, the lion himself, or the giant Egyptian with the big spear, you have a choice to make: whether to throw a pity party or make a pit stop. You can either feel persecuted and picked on, or you can use it as a chance to be refueled and retooled, revitalized and renewed.

I think of Paul and Silas in Acts 16. They were in stocks, having been beaten. And yet in that particular pit, they didn't say, 'Poor us. Here we are servants of Jesus, and look what's happened.' Rather, they sang praises to God, a miracle took place, and they were delivered.

I think of Joseph, whose brothers cast him into a literal pit in the desert and left him to die. Through a series of miracles, he eventually found himself Prime Minister of Egypt, and realized the pit into which he was cast was for the benefit of the people of God (Genesis 50:20).

I think of Daniel, who was thrown into a pit full of lions. He went into it prayerfully and as a result, Nebuchadnezzar saw the power of God released because of Daniel's victory in the pit (Daniel 7).

I find it significant that the name 'Benaiah' means 'edified'; for where was Benaiah edified, where was he built up? In the pit. So, too, may God edify, may He build you in the pit as well. In Jesus' name.

Let Down? Look Up!

*Then the disciples took him by night, and let him
down by the wall in a basket.*

Acts 9:25

THE NEWEST addition to the *New York Times* bestseller list is a book about statistics and probabilities which includes the following . . .

1 in 1,000 Americans will have murdered someone in his lifetime.

1 in 200 Americans will spend time in prison.

7 in 10 who start a company will see it go bankrupt.

9 in 10 who lose weight on a diet will gain back every pound.

The chance of being hit by lightning is 1 in 9,000.

The chance of winning the lottery is 1 in 400,000.

And the chance of being let down by someone or something is 1 in 1.

This brings us to Acts 9, where the Apostle Paul is being let down from the city wall in a basket. Initially, this must have been disconcerting, disappointing, and disillusioning for him; but Paul would later write that this time of being let down — in more ways than one — would be the second greatest event in his life. Consider the paraphrase of II Corinthians 11:30-33: The night I was lowered in a basket over the wall of Damascus was the most meaningful experience I have ever had since the day I met Christ.

Far from feeling let down by this event, Paul actually gloried in it. But it took time. You see, following his conversion, Paul's singular passion was to preach Christ to the Jews. In Romans 9:2-3, he says he would literally go to hell if it would bring about their salvation. Would you do that? Would you spend eternity in hell so your brother could be saved? I know nothing of that kind of love. Paul cared so deeply for Israel that he said he would be accursed for his brethren. Trained as a Jewish scholar and theologian, it would seem as though Paul was tailor-made as a minister to the Jews. But following Paul's conversion in Acts 9:15, God had told Ananias that Paul's ministry would be first to the Gentiles, secondly to the kings, and *lastly* to the Jews.

So what does Paul do? Acts 9:20 tells us he heads straight for the synagogues — to preach to the Jews. So poorly was he received, however, that his audience wanted to kill him, necessitating his escape by night in a basket. What does Paul do then? He heads for Jerusalem — the capital of Judaism! After spending fifteen days in Jerusalem (Galatians 1:18), Paul went into the Temple. In a trance, Paul heard the Lord say, 'I'm sending you to the Gentiles, Paul.' To which Paul answered, 'But, Lord, You're missing a great opportunity! The Jews here know I was a radical on their behalf, going into the synagogues and the homes where Christians met, to drag them out and have them killed. They know I consented to the death of Stephen, the first martyr. Don't You see, Lord, how powerful my testimony could be here in Jerusalem?' And the Lord responded by saying, 'Depart, Paul. I'm sending you to the Gentiles.' So Paul was sent to Tarsus where he would spend between seven and ten years laboring in obscurity.

Maybe you can relate to this. Maybe, like Paul, you have said, 'Lord, You're missing a great opportunity. I'm custom-made to reach these people. If You bless my business, my family, this project — Lord, just think how good it would be!' And the Lord says, 'Depart. I'm sending you somewhere else.'

'But Lord, don't You understand? If You bless this relationship, we could prosper and do such great things for You. Don't You see what You're missing, Lord?'

In Matthew 11:33, Jesus said, 'Come unto Me, all ye that labor and are heavy-laden and I will give you rest.' Rest from what? From your works, from your own plans, from trying to be religious. Four verses earlier, Jesus said, 'Take my yoke upon you, and learn of me; for I am meek and lowly in heart: and ye shall find rest unto your souls.' You see, when you come to Jesus initially, you find rest from your works. But it's only when you are yoked to Jesus that you find rest in your heart. Perhaps today you might have rest from your works — you've been born again; you're a believer — but you don't have rest in your heart. You're troubled about many things: family, finances, ministry, health, relationships.

Do you know why this is? We are troubled in our hearts when we fail to take His yoke upon us — when *we* try to call the shots and direct what *we* think should happen. Our ideas could be good, our motives noble, but not what God intends for us.

If you're troubled today because someone let you down, some project didn't open up, some relationship didn't work out, you can become a basket case — let down over the side of the wall in bitterness and defeat. Or, like Paul, you can learn to trust the Lord and see a bigger picture by saying, 'Your way, Lord, not mine. I give up. I let go. What do You want me to do? I yoke myself with You.'

What is a yoke? It's something which connects a weaker, dumber ox to a stronger, wiser ox. And guess which ox you are? 'Take My yoke upon you and learn of Me,' Jesus says to us. 'Let Me lead you.'

'But, Lord,' we say, 'we can bless people. We can see things happen! Come on, Lord.' And we try to pull God in our direction.

That's what Paul was trying to do. And it took seven to ten years before he finally gave up. Paul, the great Apostle to the Gentiles, changed the world when he accepted the yoke the Lord placed upon him and said, 'OK, we'll go in Your direction.' What if Paul hadn't learned his lesson? What if he had kept storming into synagogues, trying to make a way into Jerusalem? He would have either died at a very young age, or he would have had a very ineffective ministry.

Don't try to persuade the Lord to go your way, gang. His plan for you might be very different from your own. His vision of you might be different from the way you see yourself because people whose ministries are based upon their own abilities, skills, and talents are those who have a tendency to take the glory for themselves.

'To the Gentiles, Paul. I want to do an entirely different thing through you,' said the Lord.

'But my heart —' protested Paul.

'To the Gentiles, Paul,' answered the Lord.

'But my background —'

'To the Gentiles, Paul.'

'But my training —'

'To the Gentiles, Paul.'

'But, Lord —'

'To the Gentiles, Paul.'

'But —'

'To the Gentiles, Paul.'

'OK, Lord.'

Some of you will make this decision today. You'll finally choose to say, 'OK, Lord.' And when you do, you'll at last find rest in your soul.

The Blessedness of Brokenness

So Gideon, and the hundred men that were with him, came unto the outside of the camp in the beginning of the middle watch; and they had but newly set the watch: and they blew the trumpets, and brake the pitchers that were in their hands.

Judges 7:19

THE ODDS were absolutely brutal, yet the strategy was incredibly brilliant, as Gideon gathered 300 select soldiers and marched into battle against 135,000 Midianite men of war. Statistically, Gideon was outnumbered 450 to one. Realistically, the chances of the Israelites experiencing victory over the Midianites were about as great as that of the Los Angeles Rams beating the San Francisco 49ers today. Yet, miraculously, incredibly, the Lord gave victory to Gideon and his band of 300 men.

Here's what happened: while the Midianites snoozed in their tents in the valley below him, Gideon gave each of his men a trumpet and an earthenware pitcher, with a smoldering torch inside. Then he ordered his men to quietly surround the Midianite camp. On signal, Gideon had his men shout, 'The sword of the Lord and of Gideon,' as they smashed the pitchers, causing air to rush into the broken vessels and the smoldering embers to burst into flame. Hearing the crashing and clanging sound of broken glass, and the shouts coming from the hills around them, the Midianites came stumbling out of their tents to see torches encircling them. Since it was customary for companies of 1000 soldiers to be led by a single torch, the Midianites assumed that behind every one of the 300 torches marched a division of men. Thus, in their panic, they grabbed their swords, and, still in a sleepy stupor, began to fight one another.

An incredible story — a brilliant, God-given, inspired strategy as 300 Israeli soldiers overcame unbelievable odds to destroy 135,000 Midianites. This morning I would like us to focus on one particular segment of this story. I would like us to use stop-action, instant replay and freeze one frame. I would like us to look at a seemingly minor detail, which actually is hugely significant.

We live in a world oppressed by Midianites, dominated by Midianites, controlled by Midianites. I'm not speaking of an external race of people, but of an internal struggle within people. The dominion of Satan, the control of self, the oppression of sin is within the heart of every human being; for, like David, we are all born into sin (Psalm 51:5). We have all been tainted by sin; we have all succumbed to sin; but praise be to God, we can be liberated. We can be rescued. We can be free. God has called us into His glorious Gospel — the good news that Jesus Christ died for our sins, paid the price for all of our iniquity, rose from the dead, and wants to set up residence within our hearts — to free us, to liberate us, to lead us into life that is both abundant and eternal. That's the Gospel. And we, who have come into this saving knowledge of Jesus, are to trumpet this Gospel to all who are still dominated, controlled, and oppressed by the Midianites of sin, Satan, and self. We have the answer: the Light of the world, Jesus Christ, dwells within us. His light is inside of us — but it is also to radiate from us. And there's the rub.

You see, most of us understand that Jesus is the Light because most of us have walked in His light — and yet, all too often, His light remains inside us, all bottled up. The Lord wants to release the light of Jesus, which He has placed in you. He wants His light to shine out from you in order that others can be saved and freed and satisfied.

How does this happen? Only by breaking — for just as the light of the torch was hidden within the earthen vessel until the pitcher was broken, so, too, if our lives are going to be a blessing, there must first be a breaking. Turn to 2 Corinthians 4 where Paul capitalizes on this particular illustration . . .

> *For God, who commanded the light to shine out of darkness, hath shined in our hearts, to give the light of the knowledge of the glory of God in the face of Jesus Christ. But we have this treasure in earthen vessels, that the excellency of the power may be of God, and not of us.*
>
> *II Corinthians 4:6-7*

The light is *in* the earthen vessel. But the light cannot shine forth *from* the vessel until there is a breaking *of* the vessel.

> *We are troubled on every side, yet not distressed; we are perplexed, but not in despair; persecuted, but not forsaken; cast down, but not destroyed; always bearing about in the body the dying of the Lord Jesus, that the life also of Jesus might be made manifest in our body. For we which live are always delivered unto death for Jesus' sake, that the life also of Jesus might be made manifest in our mortal flesh. So then death worketh in us, but life in you.*
>
> *II Corinthians 4:8-12*

A Future and a Hope

This is the breaking of the vessel. What's happening in us, says Paul, is difficult on us, but necessary for you. Gang, you cannot be a blessing until you first go through breaking. Why? Because we live in a broken world.

We live in a broken world indeed. The baby in his playpen cries over a broken toy. The little boy is upset because of his broken bike. The junior higher is in agony over a broken arm. The high school sophomore is in pain because of a broken heart. The young wife is crying because of broken marriage vows. The businessman is in despair because of broken hopes. The middle-aged man is hurting because of broken health. Wherever you look, wherever you observe people, you see hurts. People are broken. People are in tough situations. And we, who have the Light and Life of Jesus Christ, can only touch them to the degree that we are able to relate to them.

I shared breakfast yesterday with a fellow who has gone through tough times. His wife left him, and took his two boys with her. As we were sharing, he related how certain people have come to him with certain ideas and understandings; and very kindly, yet very emphatically, he said, 'You know, they just don't understand. They mean well, but they don't understand. They haven't suffered. They haven't felt it. They can't relate to it.'

During times of breaking in my own life, I have observed that basically all of the people who have approached me fall into one of two categories: those who help, and those who hinder.

In thinking about people who have helped me, I have noticed a common denominator, which can be summed up in one word: brokenness. The people who were a hindrance to me with their advice, exhortations, and prophetic utterances, had not really been broken themselves. But without exception, at some point in their lives, in some area of their lives, each of those who have helped me have experienced breaking. Indeed, there's something about a broken heart, a broken spirit, a broken man, which blesses unbelievably.

Suffering Silences Satan

Brokenness. There is no other way to be effective in touching others' lives. Job knew this. He went through more breaking than any of us could possibly imagine. He lost it all, and yet it was Job's suffering which silenced Satan. You see, Satan cruised by God and said, 'Sure Job serves You. Sure he worships You. Look how You've blessed him. Look what You've given him. No wonder he walks with You. Big deal. But if those things were taken away, he would curse You. He would walk away from You' (Job 1:9-11).

When everything was taken away from Job, however, listen to how he responded:

> Behold I go forward, but he is not there; and backward, but I cannot perceive him.
>
> *Job 23:8*

Ever feel like that? Wherever you go, you can't feel or sense the Lord.

> On the left hand, where he doth work, but I cannot behold him, he hideth himself on the right hand, that I cannot see him: But he knoweth the way that I take: when he hath tried me, I shall come forth as gold.
>
> *Job 23:9-10*

'I don't know the way He's taking; I don't know what He's doing,' says Job, 'but *He* knows the way I take. *He* knows where I'm am. *He* knows what He's doing.' And with that, Satan's accusations went up in smoke.

Service Succeeds Suffering

Not only does suffering silence Satan, suffering is necessary for service.

A five-dollar iron bar can be pounded into a couple of ten-dollar horseshoes. Or, that same iron bar can be pounded further into $350 worth of needles. Or, that same iron bar can be pounded even further to produce $250,000 worth of fine watch springs. It all depends on how much pounding is done.

Maybe you feel as though you have been pounded on, worked on, and broken this week. Rejoice and be exceedingly glad, for it means God is making you into something fine, something useful, something valuable for His glory. 'I don't know about this teaching,' you say. 'I think I would rather control my own destiny than submit to the breaking of God. Thanks, but no thanks. I'll go it alone.' Those of you who, so saying, want to captain your own ship, turn with me to Acts 27 . . .

En route to Rome, where he was to stand trial before Caesar, Paul advised his shipmates they were headed for treacherous waters. Ignoring his warning, the captain sailed on — right into a storm so fierce the ship eventually ran aground before splitting into pieces. All on board were saved, however, by clinging to the broken remains of the very boat in which they were previously so proud and confident. It was the broken pieces which saved them. So, too, storms will come into your life, gang. There is not a man or woman who is exempt from this. And when they do, each of us will have a choice to make: either to flail about in our own efforts, or to grab on to the splinters and say, 'I don't have much to offer, Lord — just a bunch of shattered pieces of my life. But take control and bring me to dry land.'

If you choose the latter, guess what. The Lord will take the times of breaking, the hurts, the heartaches of your life, and He will bring not only you safely to shore; but He will use the remnants of your ship to bring others as well. You will touch, pray, and relate to people in an entirely different way — for you will have been broken.

Christian, if you're going through a time of breaking right now, know this: the process keeps going. It just keeps moving on. You might be a horseshoe, and He's making you into a needle; or you might be a needle, which He's shaping into a watch spring. Whatever you are, He's working on you, breaking you in order that the light of Jesus Christ may shine from you.

The world is impressed and blessed, moved and touched when they see people who not only rejoice and praise the Lord in times of prosperity, but who worship God and hang tough when the times are difficult; for it is then that the light of the Gospel shines forth. It is then that the trumpet of Jesus Christ is heard throughout the land. It is then that the Midianites, which oppress and depress people, are defeated.

Hang in there, gang. Don't give up. Don't question, wonder, or fret about what God is doing. 'I don't know His ways,' said Job. 'But He knows mine — and that's all that matters.'

Waiting for His Working

And so, after he had patiently endured, he obtained the promise.

Hebrews 6:15

BROKEN PROMISES produce broken hearts. Paul and Penny stand before the pastor after anticipating this day for months. They promise they'll be faithful and true in sickness or in health, in riches or rags, until death separates them. But five years later, Paul comes home and says, 'I'm out of here, Penny. You no longer meet my needs. You no longer captivate my heart.' And he walks away from the promises he made, leaving his wife and family behind.

Little Billy waits anxiously for Friday afternoon when his daddy promised to take him fishing. When the telephone rings on Friday afternoon, Billy picks it up and hears his father say, 'I'm tied up at the office, son. I can't take you fishing today. Sorry. Hope you understand.'

The Bible you hold in your hands is packed full of promises — more than 4,000 in number. Many of you have promise boxes sitting on your kitchen table, or promise books stuffed in your back pocket. But today, there are those in our midst who would say, 'My heart is broken because I don't think the Lord has kept His promise to me. I claimed the promise. I prayed it in. I wrote it on a 3x5 card and stuck it on my mirror. But nothing happened.'

Maybe, like Penny and Billy, you're in that place today. If so, this is a highly important text for you to consider. If you're not, certainly you're living near or linked to those who wonder why things don't work like Scripture promises.

In verse 12, we are exhorted to follow those who went before us and obtained the promise by faith. The author of Hebrews uses one man specifically as an illustration — Abraham, the father of faith. After Abraham patiently endured, he obtained the promise. What promise? You know the story . . .

Abraham was 75 years old when, in Genesis 12, he was told to leave his home and father to go to a new land where God would give him offspring as the stars overhead. This must have blown Abraham's mind, for he and his wife Sarah had no children at that time. Off he goes on his journey, this father of faith, and sure enough, God gave him a son from whom an entire nation was born. But it didn't happen immediately. In fact, it took 25 years. And, in this, there is a hugely important spiritual principle which needs to be part of your life: there is very often a gap of time between the promise and the performance of the promise. In Abraham's case, the gap of time was 25 years. We read that after Abraham patiently endured, he obtained the promise. I love the New Testament because it is so wonderfully gracious in that it never once mentions the sins or failings of the Old Testament saints. And that's the way God looks at you and me under the New Covenant. 'Your sins and iniquities will I remember no more,' He says (Hebrews 8:12).

If you only read the New Testament account of Abraham, you wouldn't know the rest of the story. For while it is true that Abraham patiently endured and obtained the promise, it is also true that when he was in his mid-80s, Sarah said, 'I know God promised you we would produce a nation. But let's be reasonable. Ten years have come and gone since we heard from Him — and nothing's happened. I'm long past the age of child-bearing, so have relations with my handmaid, and the child produced will count as ours.' Abraham agreed to Sarah's suggestion, and a baby named Ishmael was the result. Ishmael was not the promised child, but rather an attempt by Abraham and Sarah to try to help God fulfill His promise. And as is always the case whenever we try to help God out, Ishmael only made matters worse, for Ishmael became the father of the Arab nation. The promised son, Isaac, would come through Sarah thirteen years after Ishmael was born.

'This raises an interesting question,' you say. 'What kind of father would give a promise to his kids and then wait 25 years to fulfill it. Why does God make us wait?' Following are three reasons why God our Father tells us to patiently endure . . .

To Produce Endurance

Jeremiah was getting a bit weary of the ministry to which God called him. 'When are You going to come through, Lord?' he wondered. And God answered him by saying,

> *If thou hast run with the footmen, and they have wearied thee, then how canst thou contend with horses? and if in the land of peace, wherein thou trustedst, they wearied thee, then how wilt thou do in the swelling of Jordan?*
>
> *Jeremiah 12:5*

In other words, 'You may think it's tough now, Jeremiah, but I know what's ahead. There are some real difficulties coming your way, some tremendous challenges heading in your direction.'

Jesus made it clear that it rains on the just and the unjust alike (Matthew 5:45). *Everyone* goes through storms, folks. I don't care how spiritual you might be; you're going to go through storms. Because of the fallen condition of the world in which we live, death, disease, poverty, tragedy, and heartache abound. Consequently, God says, 'Due to the repercussions of the fall of this planet, due to the repercussions of the depravity of the race, storms are coming.'

'Change the weather,' we say.

'No,' says God. 'I am going to change *you* — through the trials you're going through right now, and through the promises you're claiming, which you have not yet seen come to fruition.'

If someone had told me twenty years ago the things that would come down in my life, I would have said, 'I can't deal with that. I won't be a part of that. No way.' But my Father has been so good, so faithful to prepare me all along the way through difficulties and challenges. Yes, there were promises, but there were gaps between the promise and performance, which tested my faith — not because God was cruel to me, but because He cared about me. 'I'm training you for what I see is coming down the path,' He said. It's all part of the plan, son.'

To Perfect Blessing

'I'm going to do exceeding abundantly above all you could ask or even think,' the Lord says (Ephesians 3:20) — 'but it's going to take time.'

WAITING FOR HIS WORKING

Due to his allergies, when my son, Peter John, was a baby, he required a special formula. On one of the very rare occasions when I was up at night with him, he started crying as I impatiently heated his bottle. I can remember saying, 'Calm down, buddy. It's coming. You won't want it cold.' But you know what? He continued to howl because he couldn't understand what I was saying. And the Lord whispered in my ear that night, 'Jon, that's you. I'm cooking something up; I'm getting something ready. But you're crying 'Where is it?' because you don't understand the language of faith.' And that's all of us. 'Wah, wah,' we cry. 'It's been twenty-five days, two years, or fifteen years. Where's the promise?' And all along, the Father is saying, 'I'm getting it ready. I'm going to do something better than you could even imagine. But it's going to take some time.'

Zacharias and Elizabeth were well beyond the years of bearing children. No doubt they had stopped asking for children decades ago. But God heard them, and knew He not only wanted to give them a baby, but He wanted to give them the greatest prophet who had ever lived, one who would prepare the hearts of Israel for the coming of His Son (Luke 1:16). The same is true for you and me today. God says, 'I want to do things beyond anything you could dream or imagine. So hang on, folks, the bottle's getting warm.'

I have discovered that the longer God takes to fulfill a promise in my life, oftentimes, the better it will be. 'I want a man who loves God passionately,' she says. 'Doesn't God say to delight in Him and He'll give us the desire of our hearts? Well, I'm praying for a man who loves God, who's 6'4" with dark hair, a big smile, and a good business head; who loves to talk about the Lord; who cares about people; who's a good athlete with a great sense of humor; who's sensitive and considerate; and who has eyes only for me. That's what I want.' So the Lord begins shaping and developing her to make her the woman who would be attractive to the man of her desires. But what do we say?

'I've waited two months,' as we head off to Rockin' Rodeo to scope out the situation. And we wonder why we end up with Tex.

After Abraham patiently endured, he obtained the promise. We know the inside story. He didn't patiently endure perfectly. But he learned his lesson, and the promise eventually came his way.

To Prepare Us

The language of eternity is faith. When the Lord has us ruling and reigning at His side, under His command, doing His bidding — whatever that means in the ages to come — He's going to need men and women like you, who are not second-guessing, not doubting, not faltering. Jesus taught about the faithful in this life who will be rulers over five and ten cities in the Kingdom (Luke 19).

In other words, Jesus is saying there is a destiny far beyond what any of us know or can imagine awaiting us in the next zillion years to come. And the language which must be fluently spoken by us, if we are to be ambassadors for Him in the realms and regions beyond, is the language of faith.

She was the best teacher I ever had. We walked in to our sophomore Spanish class, and Senorita Thomas greeted us that first day saying, 'Listen, carefully. These are the last words of English you're going to hear the entire year in this class.' And that was it. From then on, everything she spoke was Spanish. It was miserable initially. But it forced us to think in a way we never would have if we had been able to fall back on English.

And that's what the Father's doing. 'Kids,' He says, 'the only way you'll be prepared for what's coming is if I force you to learn the language of faith now because that's the language you'll be speaking for the next billion years to come.'

If I were God, do you know what I'd do? Once a year, I'd go to every church and appear with a great display of power and fire and smoke. That would probably get everyone by for a year or so. But God knows such a thing would actually undo what He desires to do, for the growth of faith would be retarded. We would depend on what we could see physically or hear audibly; and consequently, we would not be fluent in the language of eternity.

All of the promises will come about in due season. In the meantime, precious people, realize God's heating the bottle. Understand that He's forcing you to develop a whole new way of thinking and living.

'OK,' you might be saying. 'I see the blessings of waiting. But what do I do *while* I'm waiting?' Turn to Isaiah 40 . . .

> *But they that wait upon the Lord shall renew*
> *their strength; they shall mount up with wings as*

eagles; they shall run, and not be weary; they shall walk, and not faint.

Isaiah 40:31

In the day when you are feeling frustrated or fatigued, don't fight but rather flow. And wait on the Lord. Please notice, we're not told to wait *for* the Lord. We're to wait *on* the Lord. And there's a world of difference between the two. A good waiter in a restaurant doesn't just wait for you to finish your meal. He serves, tends, and seeks to please you. So, too, when you feel faint or fried, wait on the Lord. Say, 'I'm going to take my eyes off the trouble which threatens me, the problems which surround me, and wait on my Lord. When the sun comes up, I'll welcome Him to the day, worship Him, and spend time listening to Him speak to me through His Word. As I go through the day, instead of complaining and worrying, I'll wait on the Lord and magnify Him through worship and praise.'

Those who wait on the Lord with the intent of bringing pleasure to Him shall indeed mount up with wings as eagles — they'll fly high. They'll run and not be weary — as they'll keep going, never slowing down, never quitting. They'll walk and not faint — even in the mundane daily paths which so often wear others down.

Wait on the Lord, saint. No matter what you go through, may you embrace the trials as being from Him, and may you experience afresh the love, and peace that come as you wait on Him. He'll comfort you, gang. He did me, and He will you, for He's true to His Word.

Don't Jump Ship

Paul said to the centurion and to the soldiers, Except these abide in the ship, ye cannot be saved. Then the soldiers cut off the ropes of the boat, and let her fall off.

Acts 27:31-32

AFTER JUMPING through legal hoops in Caesarea, Paul was finally sailing towards Rome to plead his case before Caesar. On the way, a storm arose which threatened the lives of the 275 soldiers, sailors and prisoners on board with him. After the crew readied a lifeboat to avoid the inevitable dashing of the ship against the rocks, Paul, the little rabbi who was a tentmaker by trade and a prisoner by decree, said, 'Except ye abide in the ship, ye cannot be saved' (Acts 27:31). I believe Paul's words are the heart of the Lord for us today. There are times — maybe you're in one right now — when the wind is howling, the waves are rising, and you find yourself saying, 'That's it. I'm out of here. I'm jumping ship . . .

I can't take this marriage one more day.

I can't take this job one more hour.

I can't take my parents one more minute. '

Storms come, and the temptation arises within all of us to bail out when we think we've been tricked or cheated. I share with you the story of a man who truly had reason to feel this way. His name is Jacob, and his story begins in the 29th chapter of the book of Genesis . . .

Jacob was young, single, footloose, and looking for a wife. Arriving in Pandanaram, he found a group of shepherds milling around a well. Industrious by nature,

Jacob couldn't understand this — until he saw a beautiful shepherdess approaching, bringing her flock with her. Immediately, Jacob flexed his muscles, single-handedly removed the stone which covered the well, and gallantly said, 'Come and water your flock.' She did, he kissed her, and then he cried aloud, for she had smitten his heart.

When Jacob discovered this beautiful maiden was the daughter of his uncle, he went to her father and said, 'I want to marry your daughter.

'OK,' said Laban. 'Work for me seven years, and I'll give her to you.' Jacob agreed, and the Bible says it seemed to him but a few days because of the great love he had for her.

The big night finally came. Jacob took his beloved bride — veiled from head to toe according to Jewish tradition — to his tent where they consummated the marriage. The next morning, when Jacob opened his eyes, he couldn't believe what he saw; for it wasn't Rachel he had married — it was her older sister, Leah. Jacob stormed out of the tent, found Laban, and said, 'You tricked me.'

'I'm sorry, Jacob,' his uncle said, 'but we have a custom that the older daughter must marry before the younger daughter. But I'll tell you what I'll do. Work seven more years, and I'll throw in Rachel.'

Now if anyone ever had a right to say, 'I got tricked — I want out,' it was Jacob. 'Listen, Leah,' he could have said, 'I realize we went through the ceremony, but I didn't know who you were. I'm in love with Rachel. So I'm out of here.' But that's not what Jacob did. He agreed to Laban's proposal, and thus ended up with both Leah and Rachel as his wives. Time passed. Between Leah, Rachel, and their handmaidens, Jacob fathered twelve sons, who became, of course, the twelve tribes of Israel. In the birth of the youngest, Rachel died, and Jacob buried this one about whom he was so passionate in Canaan. Years later, Leah died, and Jacob buried her in the Promised Land, in a place called Machpelah.

In Genesis 49, when Jacob was about to die as an old man, he called his twelve sons together and after blessing each one said, 'I am going the way of my fathers. When I die, bury me at —. Now, I would have thought he would have said, 'Bury me by the love of my life. Bury me by Rachel.' But that's not what he said. He said, 'Bury me at Machpelah — by Leah.' Why would he say that? Because at the end of his life, Jacob realized that what he thought was a trick, a gyp, unfair, was in reality the biggest blessing in his life because from Leah — not Rachel — came Judah. And from the tribe of Judah came the Messiah, Jesus Christ.

Wife, you might look at the man next to you and say, 'I was tricked. He's not the man I thought he would be.' Husband, you might look at the woman you married and say, 'She's not the passion of my life. I didn't know she would turn out this way.' But if you jump ship, know this — if you bail out, understand this: You will miss the blessing of the birthing of Jesus in a supernatural, incredible, wonderful way because there are no tricks in the life of a child of God.

Employee, you might look at your boss and say, 'When I signed that contract, I didn't know he would be such a jerk. I don't care what I signed. I'm going to find a legal loophole. I'm jumping ship.' But when you put pen to paper and signed your name, your Father was there. And to the child of God, there are no tricks.

Teenager, you might look at your parents and say, 'I was tricked. I must have been switched at birth. God couldn't have chosen *these* people to raise me.' But know this: You are not only their child — you are a child of the King. He, in His wisdom, handpicked them for you, and He makes no mistakes.

Paul said, 'If you jump ship, you'll lose your life.' And the centurion, knowing how tempting it would be for the sailors to bail out, to jump ship, to give up, ordered the soldiers to cut the lines so there would be no possibility of escape.

Maybe you're saying, 'I haven't jumped ship. I've only lowered a lifeboat over the side. I'll give it three more months, or two more weeks, or one more year.' But if you keep an escape option open in your mind, I guarantee you will end up using it. Think about divorce, and you'll jump ship. Think about changing jobs, and you'll bail out. Think about leaving home, and you'll never see His reality. Get rid of the lifeboats. Cut the lines.

'It's easy for you to pontificate,' you say. 'You don't know the storm I'm in. You don't know how vehemently the wind is blowing, how violently the waves are pounding. You just don't understand.' You're right. I don't. But there is One who does . . .

In 1902, a fire broke out, which flared up rapidly in the home of an elderly woman. Asleep in the upstairs bedroom was her grandson, whom she tried to rescue before she died in the process. Someone outside heard the screams of the five-year-old boy, however, and found a way to climb hand-over-hand up a drainpipe until he made it to the roof, broke through a window, and pulled the boy out to safety.

This story, which appeared in the *St. Louis Globe Herald*, generated quite a bit of interest in the orphaned boy. During the hearings which followed, a schoolteacher came forward and gave reasons why he felt he should be appointed the boy's guardian. So did a wealthy businessman, a minister, and several other upstanding people of the community. The boy, however, looked down and never raised his eyes until a man came through the back doors of the courtroom, walked up to him, and opened his hands. The boy looked at the charred and badly blistered hands of the stranger, and jumped into his arms saying, 'This will be my dad.'

So, too, I'm asking you to look at the hands of One who loves you so much that He absorbed the heat of hell to pull you out of eternal destruction. I'm asking you to listen to this One who says, 'Trust Me. Don't jump ship, or all will be lost.'

Precious people, Jesus will come in a way that will blow your mind if you don't jump ship. Ignore what the sailors of society are saying about breaking commitments, bailing out, giving up. Cut the ropes. Let the lifeboat crash in the sea below. Stay on board and, like Jacob, you'll look back and see in Leah was the blessing all along.

Thinking of You

For I know the thoughts that I think toward you,
saith the Lord, thoughts of peace, and not of evil,
to give you an expected end.

Jeremiah 29:11

ON OUR way to a day of skiing at Mt. Bachelor, in the spring of 1982, I told my wife, Terry, a joke. We laughed, and then suddenly our car hit ice, spun around and hit a redwood tree. My beautiful wife died right next to me. We were both 29. The next thing I remember is crawling down Highway 42 about a half-mile from the wreck on my hands and knees. Being very early morning, no cars were on the road. The first car that came stopped, and the driver called an ambulance. I don't remember anything after that until I was in the ambulance.

'How's my wife?' I asked.

'She's doing fine,' said the ambulance attendant.

'No,' I said. 'She's in heaven.'

'You're right,' he said. 'She's not with us any longer.'

At that moment, something happened to me that had only happened a few times in my life. I heard what seemed to be an audible voice, speaking to me a verse I had never heard: 'I know the thoughts I think toward you, thoughts of peace and not of evil, to bring you to a glorious end.' After that, I drifted into unconsciousness.

In the hospital, the voice on the other end of the phone was Chuck Smith's, saying, 'Jon, I have one thing to share with you. God would say: I know the thoughts I think toward you, thoughts of peace and not of evil, to bring you to a glorious end.' The very verse I had heard in the ambulance was now being spoken into my ear by my pastor.

I clung to God's promise of Jeremiah 29:11 that first hour after Terry had been taken. And for the following three years as Christy, not yet two; Jessie, just three; and Peter John, almost five; were carried along with me into a foreign land of new experiences, God proved to be faithful to His Word . . .

Recently, the woman sitting next to me on the flight home from Chicago, where I had been speaking at a Men's Retreat, was planning to move from Cape Cod to the Oregon Coast.

'Is Gold Beach like Boston?' she asked.

'No,' I said, 'there's quite a big difference between the two,' and went on to share with her the blessings of living in Oregon. 'It's a great place to raise a family,' I continued. 'In fact, I just happen to have some pictures of my family with me,' I said, opening my backpack.

'These are my kids, and this is my beautiful wife,' I said proudly. 'The Lord has blessed me so much with her. She's absolutely perfect for me.' And as I continued to talk about my family, tears came to my eyes because the photographs I held in my hand were pictures not only of Tammy and the kids, but of the expected end to which God had so lovingly, graciously, and faithfully brought us.

For over 40 years, Jeremiah faithfully proclaimed this word from God to His people: The Babylonians are coming, and will carry you away to a foreign land. Yet, although the people rejected Jeremiah's message in favor of those who predicted peace and prosperity, the Lord continued to speak through him, saying, 'When you find yourselves in the land of Babylon, I don't want you to be confused. I want you to know that My thoughts towards you are not of evil, but of peace — to bring you to a certain end.'

What was this end? We know from studying the full counsel of Scripture that there were three reasons the Lord allowed His people to be carried into captivity . . .

To Eradicate Idolatry

The Jews had a tendency to persist in the worship of idols and all that went along with it — the immoral, sexual acts, the murder of children, the offering of human sacrifices, the open worship of Satan. Therefore, because of their fascination with idolatry, the Lord allowed them to be carried away to Babylon, where they would worship idols day and night until they got sick of them . . .

During the time I was raising my kids alone, I had a problem with a particular addiction. One late night, while my kids were asleep, I gave in to my irresistible craving when I opened the refrigerator and scooped a big spoonful of Adam's Chunky Peanut Butter out of a jar. I savored the taste as I popped it in my mouth — but this time, instead of sliding down my throat as it had always done before, the peanut butter got stuck.

Gasping for air, I threw open the refrigerator door, grabbed a gallon of milk, and started chugging. But instead of washing the peanut butter down, the milk took the path of least resistance, flowing down my beard and all over my chest. At this point, I could envision my kids getting up in the morning to find me laying on the kitchen floor, covered with milk and peanut butter. Finally, in somewhat of a daze, I put my mouth under the faucet of the kitchen sink and turned on the hot water. Although my lips were scalded in the process, I could breathe again. I was thus delivered from my addiction!

So, too, in allowing His people to go to Babylon, the Lord was, in effect, saying, 'If this is what it takes for you to get your fill of idols, go to Babylon for 70 years in order that you might come back and love Me with your whole heart' (Jeremiah 24:7). And guess what. Upon their return from Babylon, the Jews never again had a pull towards idolatry, even to this day.

To Evangelize Effectively

God blessed a specific group of people, in a specific corner of the world, because He wanted the rest of the world to see that if people would walk with God, then He would bless them. The Jews were to be a witness to the world of what God will do for those who walk with Him. But what happened? The Jews became selfish and inward, and actually put down those whom they should have been reaching. So, as the Lord often has done throughout history, He had them scattered. They were taken to Babylon — a land to which they would never have gone otherwise.

Were the Jews a witness there? Refusing to bow down to the statue Nebuchadnezzar built, three young Jewish men, Shadrach, Meshach, and Abednego, were thrown into a fiery furnace. Do you think they were witnesses to Nebuchadnezzar as he watched them standing with Jesus in the fire? (Daniel 4:25). Do you think Belshazzar was blown away when one of the Jewish captives named Daniel interpreted the writing on the wall, which had been inscribed by a mysterious hand? (Daniel 5:14). Do you think the Babylonian officials were shocked when, after spending a night in the lions' den, Daniel emerged unharmed? (Daniel 7:22). The entire Book of Daniel is the story of how God used His people, who were in captivity, to witness to the Babylonians in order that they might see the reality of Jehovah, the God of Israel.

To Restore the Land Physically

In II Chronicles 36, God told the Jews that every seventh year was to be a Sabbath year. They were to do no planting, no agricultural work whatsoever, in order that the land might rest. 'In the sixth year, I'll bless you twofold,' God said, 'which will allow you to replenish the land in the seventh year.'

'Hmm,' thought the Jews. 'If we get blessed the sixth year, what would happen if we planted the seventh year as well? We could pay our bills, rid ourselves of our MasterCard payments, get a whole bunch of new stuff, and really get ahead.' So, guess what they did? For 490 years, they planted crops and harvested in the Sabbath year when the land should have been resting.

But all the while God was noticing. 'You robbed this land and you robbed Me of 70 years,' He said. 'Consequently, while you are in Babylon, I will refresh the land physically and balance the books on you nationally.' So it was that, as the Jews were carried away to Babylon, their land basically sat idle and replenished itself during their 70-year absence. 'Even as you are carried into captivity,' says God to His people, 'know this — and as you are in Babylon, remember this: My thoughts toward you are not of evil, but of peace, to bring you to an expected end that you might be liberated from idolatry, that you might witness evangelistically that your land might be refreshed physically. I'm doing this for your benefit because I love you.'

> *How precious also are thy thoughts unto me, O God! how great is the sum of them! If I should count them, they are more in number than the sand: when I awake, I am still with thee.*
>
> *Psalm 139:17-18*

When people from our fellowship vacation in some exotic place like Hawaii or Europe and send me postcards, which say, 'Wish you were here. Thinking of you.' I know they're not. I don't mean to sound cynical, but who of us thinks about his pastor when he's on a beautiful beach enjoying the sun? Not so with God. His thoughts toward us are more in number than the grains of sand on the seashore.

Scientists estimate that there are 10 to the 22nd power — that is, a one with 22 zeros after it, or one hundred billion times one hundred billion — grains of sand. 'One hundred billion times one hundred billion — that's how many times I think of you,' says God. 'You are always on My mind and on My heart. And as I think of you, My thoughts toward you are of peace, to give you an expected end.'

During one of our 'Prophecy Update' retreats, I sent the retreatants out on the grounds of the mountaintop to contemplate Revelation 6-19. My daughter was there — as she seemed to always be — and when everyone gathered to share insights, she said, 'Dad, I noticed the seven bowl judgments correspond perfectly with the seven sayings Christ made on the Cross as He absorbed the judgment which should have been ours.' That's the way Jessie was. She loved the Word, and she loved the Lord.

Thus, at 6:30 AM, as I sat toward the back of the sanctuary during morning worship, it was no surprise to see my daughter walk in and sit towards the front. After a few worship songs, Rick invited folks to lead out in prayer. Several people prayed, and then my daughter stood up and said, 'Lord, I thank You for the promise in Your Word that says the thoughts You think toward us are thoughts of peace, and not of evil, to bring us to a glorious end.' Jessie didn't know the personal relevance of that verse to me. But Rick understood, and he immediately penned a song, which he sang that morning during Communion. After kneeling at Communion, Jessie walked up the aisle, smiled at me, and gave the 'thumbs up' sign as she headed off to school.

Twenty minutes later, one of the pastors came in the Sanctuary and said, 'Jon, there's been a wreck. It's a yellow Volkswagen. We're not sure yet, but we think it's Jessie.'

'No,' I said. 'That can't be. I've already been through this once.'

I jumped in my car and raced home, thinking it was a mistake. But as I walked in the door and saw Tammy, I knew it wasn't. One of the first at the scene of the accident, my son, Peter John, walked in a few minutes later, sobbing, 'She found the Man, Dad. She found the

Man.' You see, the night before, Jessie, Christy, and I were talking about boyfriends and marriage and stuff like that. 'Jessie,' I had said, 'you need to find someone who can lead you spiritually — not just a Christian guy, not just someone who loves the Lord, but someone who can *lead* you.'

Quick-witted as always, Jessie said, 'Where am I going to find that man, Dad? I mean, if I went to a good church, I'd have a chance, but . . . '

I cracked up, and said, 'Jessie, you'll find him. Just don't settle for anything less than a man who can lead you in the ways of God.'

Having heard part of this conversation, Peter John knew she had found the One who could truly lead her.

Every January our high school youth group kids write letters to themselves containing their goals for the upcoming year. The following January these letters are mailed so the kids can see how the Lord has worked in their lives the previous year. Two months after Jessie went to heaven there was such a letter in our mailbox addressed to her. Understandably, with hundreds of letters, no one thought to pull hers out. As tears flowed, Tammy and I opened it to find the question: If Jesus could do one thing for you in 1994, what would it be? Like her father, Jessie was never at a loss for words. Therefore, it was surprising to see her answer was only five words long: to take me to heaven.

Leader of her school and youth group, cheerleader and straight-A student, Jessie loved life. But she had a greater Love than life — she loved Jesus immensely. I'm sure Jessie was thinking about the Rapture, but the Lord saw her heart and had a private Rapture just for her, and did *indeed* bring her to an expected, glorious end.

Precious brother and sister — even if you feel like you're being held captive in Babylon; even if you feel as though you're walking through a foreign land; even if you wonder what's happening in your job, your marriage, your life — embrace the promise of the One who spoke peace even to a people who ignored and rebelled against Him. He's bringing you to an expected end, dear people of God. You might not see it now, but His thoughts toward you are truly of peace, to bring you to an expected end — to bring you to Himself.